TAXATION IN BRITAIN SINCE 1660

Taxation in Britain since 1660

Roy Douglas
Emeritus Reader
University of Surrey

First published in Great Britain 1999 by
MACMILLAN PRESS LTD
Houndmills, Basingstoke, Hampshire RG21 6XS and London
Companies and representatives throughout the world

A catalogue record for this book is available from the British Library.

ISBN 0–333–67364–6

First published in the United States of America 1999 by
ST. MARTIN'S PRESS, INC.,
Scholarly and Reference Division,
175 Fifth Avenue, New York, N.Y. 10010

ISBN 0–312–22217–3

Library of Congress Cataloging-in-Publication Data
Douglas, Roy.
Taxation in Britain since 1600 / Roy Douglas.
p. cm.
Includes bibliographical references and index.
ISBN 0–312–22217–3 (cloth)
1. Taxation—Great Britain—History. I. Title.
HJ2603.D68 1999
336.2'00941—dc21   99–18160
                                                      CIP

*HJ
2603
.D68
1999*

This book is printed on paper suitable for recycling and made from fully managed and
sustained forest sources.

10   9   8   7   6   5   4   3   2   1
08 07 06 05 04 03 02 01 00 99

Printed and bound in Great Britain by
Antony Rowe Ltd, Chippenham, Wiltshire

Contents

List of Figures

Acknowledgements

The author wishes to express grateful thanks to his wife Jean and to David Mills for their helpful comments on the manuscript.

He also wishes to thank the British Museum and the British Library for permission to reproduce the figures indicated in the list on p. vii.

Chronology

1795	Introduction of 'Speenhamland system' of pauper relief in Berkshire, soon adopted in many other counties.
1798	Great increase in 'Assessed Taxes'. Provision for redemption of taxpayers' liability for 'Land Tax'.
1799	Income Tax introduced.
1801	Union between Great Britain and Ireland. Pitt resigns; succeeded by Addington.
1802	'Peace of Amiens'. Income Tax abolished.
1803	War with France resumed. Income Tax restored.
1804	Pitt becomes 'Prime Minister' again.
1806	Death of Pitt.
1815	Battle of Waterloo. End of French Wars.
1816	Income Tax abolished.
1825	Abolition of remaining salt duties.
1832	'Great Reform Act' results in substantial increase in electorate and abolition of the worst 'rotten boroughs'.
1833	Abolition of slavery throughout British Empire. Incorporation of Scottish Burghs with elective authorities. Similar legislation later applied to England and Wales (1835) and Ireland (1840).
1834	Poor Law Amendment Act for England and Wales establishes 'workhouse test' for recipients of poor relief.
1842	Budget of Sir Robert Peel results in abolition or reduction of many customs duties, and reintroduction of Income Tax.
1845	Beginning of Irish Famine.
1846	Repeal of Corn Laws.
1853	Gladstone's first Budget. Many further reductions in indirect taxes, including abolition of soap duties. Abolition of Irish Poor Law debts occasioned by the Famine, but introduction of Income Tax in Ireland.
1854	'Crimean War' begins.
1860	Cobden's treaty with France. Another Gladstone budget results in abolition of protective duties.
1861	Abolition of paper duties.
1867	Further extension of franchise.
1872	Secret ballot.
1879	Exceptionally wet summer precipitates long-term agricultural crisis. Publication of Henry George's *Progress and Poverty* stimulates radical thinking about distribution of wealth and relation to land question.
1884–5	'Household franchise'.
1888	Establishment of County Councils.
1891	Elementary education becomes free as well as universal.
1894	Sir William Harcourt's budget abolishes distinction between realty and personalty for inheritance purposes, and introduces graduated inheritance taxation. Establishment of District and Parish Councils.
1899–1902	Boer War.
1903	Commencement of Joseph Chamberlain's 'Tariff Reform' campaign.
1906	(January/February) General Election gives new Liberal Government large majority, vindicating Free Trade policy. Parliamentary Labour Party established.

1908	Introduction of Old Age Pensions.

1908   Introduction of Old Age Pensions.

1909   First Lloyd George budget. Proposals include land valuation and taxation; Income Tax graduation; introduction of Super Tax (later known as Surtax). Budget rejected by House of Lords.

1910   After January General Election, 1909 budget proposals accepted.

1911   Parliament Act removes power of House of Lords to reject Money Bills, and reduces power of House of Lords to reject other bills. National Insurance Act passed.

1914   Outbreak of First World War followed by massive and repeated increases in taxation.

1915   First Coalition Government (Asquith). Introduction of McKenna Duties.

1916   Second Coalition Government (Lloyd George).

1918   Armistice. New General Election confirms Lloyd George Coalition in office.

1919   Austen Chamberlain budget adapts McKenna Duties to policy of Imperial Preference.

1920   Abolition of Land Taxes and land valuation.

1922   All taxation powers of UK Parliament over most of Ireland renounced. Fall of Coalition.

1929   Great Depression begins in US.

1931   National Government formed. Large increases in taxation and reductions in unemployment benefit.

1932   General policy of protective tariffs adopted.

1933   Failure of Disarmament Conference, followed by gradual introduction of rearmament and increased taxation.

1937   Defence Loans Act authorises rearmament financing through increases in National Debt.

1939   Outbreak of Second World War followed by repeated further taxation increases.

1940   National Government replaced by Coalition Government (Churchill). Introduction of Purchase Tax.

1942   Beveridge Report.

1944   Income Tax PAYE comes into effect.

1945   End of Second World War. Labour Government replaces Coalition government.

1946   National Insurance and National Health Acts.

1951   Rearmament consequential on Korean War leads to taxation increases and introduction of National Health charges.

1965–6. Capital Gains Tax, Selective Employment Tax (SET) and Corporation Tax introduction.

1971–3   UK joins EEC (1973). SET reduced, later abolished. Purchase Tax phased out, replaced by VAT. Surtax abolished.

1975   Unemployment begins to rise substantially. Petroleum Revenue Tax (PRT) introduced; yield becomes substantial in 1978–9.

1979   Margaret Thatcher Prime Minister. Rapid further increase in unemployment. Sir Geoffrey Howe's Budget results in decrease in Income Tax (continued in subsequent years), but increase of VAT to 15 per cent and increase in PRT. Rapid increase in PRT yield.

xii Chronology

1989	Community Charge ('Poll Tax') applied to local authorities in Scotland.
1990	Community Charge and UBR applied to England and Wales. Great shortfall in anticipated revenue. Fall of Thatcher.
1991–2.	Replacement of Community Charge by Council Tax. VAT increased.
1997	Labour Government (Tony Blair).

1 Restoration

When Charles II returned to England to claim the throne in May 1660, public finance was in a state of considerable confusion. There was much debate about what taxes ought to be levied and how they should be collected.

There was nothing new about that. An important strand in the history of the seventeenth century, and of the previous century as well, is the expedients used by successive rulers to raise revenue they needed, and the reactions of people who thought that they would lose out in consequence.

One might almost say that nobody had really found a replacement for feudalism, which had been slowly disintegrating over several centuries. Feudalism had been a system of reciprocal rights and duties, pivoting on the ownership of land. Through feudalism, the main ordinary requirements of government had once been provided. All land belonged, in law, to the King. Some of that land was part of the King's personal estate from which he derived revenue. Other pieces of land were held by 'tenants', who paid the Sovereign for the privilege by various kinds of services – which, as time went on, were usually commuted for money. By the seventeenth century, feudalism was almost extinct, but the King still maintained substantial estates where, for practical purposes, he was in more or less the same position as any other great landlord.

The cry, 'The King should live of his own!' was occasionally raised in the seventeenth century. This meant that the King should rely exclusively on revenues from the Royal estates and those feudal dues which still survived, to which might perhaps be added the grant of customs duties which Parliament had made more or less automatically at the beginning of each reign, for a very long time.

The demand was more hopeful than realistic. In practice, the King nearly always needed revenue from other sources, most particularly to defray the cost of foreign wars. Kings were often conspicuously less enthusiastic for those wars than were the leading statesmen.

Beyond his personal resources, the King could obtain money from either Parliament or exercise of the Royal Prerogative. The Prerogative was – and is – the powers which at Common Law are personal to the Sovereign. Those powers cover a good deal more than finance, but it was the King's financial powers which were of critical importance.

In the first part of the seventeenth century, there had been a long, complex argument as to how far the King could lawfully raise the revenue he required through exercise of the Prerogative. Could he, for example,

Figure 1   For a period at the turn of the seventeenth and eighteenth centuries, playing cards were sometimes used as the vehicle of political satire. Most of the cards in this set refer to incidents in the reign of James II, but this one relates to the

require subjects who were living in inland counties to pay Ship Money for naval defence? Could he impose indirect taxes on goods as he pleased? Could he give – or sell – monopolies over various kinds of trade to selected individuals or corporations? Could he enforce 'benevolences' and forced loans on his subjects? If he could do all these things, then he would be, financially, more or less a free agent, for there would be no need for him to go to Parliament for money.

Parliament thought otherwise; and the struggle between King and Parliament over control of public finance was a large element, though certainly not the only element, in the genesis of the Civil War. Parliamentarians understood very clearly that if they had control over taxation, they could require the King to do more or less whatever they desired on other matters.

When one considers 'Parliaments' of this period, it is important to avoid the nineteenth-century fallacy of writing history backwards and perceiving those Parliaments as representing in some way the views and the will of the ordinary people of the country. Seventeenth-century Parliaments, whether Royalist or republican in their ideology, represented only a tiny minority of the people. The power of the wealthier classes, and most particularly of those whose wealth derived from hereditary ownership of land, was dominant in the House of Commons and the House of Lords alike. From the fifteenth century onwards, the power and influence of men whose wealth was drawn from trade, manufacture or finance had grown rapidly; but those people graded insensibly into the traditional landed classes.

What impresses the modern reader most sharply about seventeenth-century methods of raising or spending money is their haphazard nature. Until the middle of the century, the modern idea that Government spending

---

(*Figure caption continued*)
reign of his brother. The King is receiving bags of money from Louis XIV, and the text reads:

'500 thousand pound sent from France yearly to Charls the 2 to keep the sitting of the Parlement of.'

This refers to the 'Secret Treaty of Dover' of 1670, by which Charles II received substantial sums from the French King, undertaking eventually to announce his conversion to the Catholic faith. That agreement was followed by others between the two monarchs. The sum stated on the card is a gross exaggeration of what Charles received. The true sum, which has been stated to average £123,664 a year, would certainly not be enough to avert the need to summon Parliament. There is no doubt, however, that Charles II was anxious to discover sources of revenue which would make him independent of taxation, for which Parliamentary authority would be essential.

should be anticipated and provided for was seldom seriously considered, let alone followed. There were several traditional kinds of taxation designed to meet the needs of government.

The most regular and familiar of these methods was through customs duties. Customs were of mediaeval origin. Originally, they constituted a levy on both imports and exports, collected – at least in theory – in order to enable the King to maintain a navy which would protect traders from the depradations of pirates and foreign enemies. The right to levy customs was normally granted by Parliament to the King at the beginning of his reign and remained with him for life. As a regular and continuing source of income, customs were exceedingly useful to the King. The sums collected represented a very substantial proportion of the total Royal revenue.[1]

During the earlier part of the seventeenth century, the character of customs had been changing in several ways. The specific association of the duties with the provision of a navy was being gradually eroded, and they were becoming assimilated in the general volume of taxation – although Acts of Parliament throughout the century continued to emphasise the formal link with naval defence. Additional customs duties were imposed from time to time to meet special requirements. Duties on exported goods were slowly abandoned, but a few persisted for long afterwards. Even in the seventeenth century, some people were coming to see customs not only as a source of revenue, but also as a means for regulating external trade.

Today, customs and excise are often mentioned in one breath; but the origin of excise duties was much more recent. They were introduced in 1643 by John Pym and were extended in the next few years. Excise duties were imposed largely on items regarded as necessities, and mainly on goods of domestic origin. These included such commodities as beer, cider, meat, salt, starch and hats. As time went on, the excise duties on beer became particularly important. When Charles II returned from exile, most counties and towns were operating a system of tax-farming for excise.[2] Government Commissioners for Appeals were appointed to supervise the activities of the tax-farmers. As with customs, extra excise duties were applied in times of perceived need.

Direct taxes also formed an important source of revenue. Unlike customs duties, they had traditionally been levied as emergency measures only, to meet some special need, usually a war, and Parliamentary authority was required. Before the mid-seventeenth century turmoil, taxes known as 'fifteenths and tenths' had occasionally been levied at an assessment based on the taxpayer's personal wealth. The sum was related, however, to an ancient valuation, and the effect of subsequent inflation was to render the yield derisory. Another traditional direct tax was the 'subsidy'. This was levied at the rate of 4 shillings in the pound (20 per cent) on 'land' and 2s 8d (13.3 per cent) on personal property. The word 'land' was understood in the lawyer's sense of the word to include not only the site itself – that is, 'land' in the classical economist's sense – but also improvements, such as buildings or crops, which had been put on it by human agency. Inflation had also greatly reduced the yield of the 'subsidy'.[3] From time to time, various other taxes were introduced; but most of these were soon abandoned.

During the Civil War and Commonwealth period, the old 'fifteenths and tenths' and 'subsidies' were abandoned and replaced by a new kind to direct taxation. Parliament fixed the tax liability of a county or borough, and prominent local men were appointed to collect the assessed sum from property owners in the area. These 'assessments' were made at frequent intervals – originally weekly, but later monthly.

The collectors then passed the tax to the Receivers-General, who financed the army directly, without passing the money through the Exchequer. Various kinds of goods and certain salaries were assessed; but, in practice, the 'Assessment' taxes were levied mainly on landed estates.[4] To this point it will be necessary to return later. Farmers and yeomen were charged not on the basis of their income but on the rental value of their holdings.[5] The new 'Assessment' taxes, conjoined with the old customs duties and the new excise duties, were the three principal sources of revenue during the commonwealth, and were ready in place at the time of the Restoration of the monarchy under Charles II.

Even before the Restoration, fundamental questions were beginning to be raised about the wisdom and the morality of various kinds of taxation; the debate would continue for a long time to come.[6] Indirect taxes were usually simpler to collect than direct taxes. If the government required to obtain customs duties on luxury imports, it was only necessary to watch a relatively small number of ports. If the government sought to collect excise on beer, it was fairly easy to identify a relatively small number of brewers and require them to give sums of money to excise collectors in anticipation of future sales.

Of course, these controls would not be completely effective. Some brandy would be landed at obscure coves at dead of night and would find its way to the ultimate consumer without duty being paid. Some people would brew untaxed beer and sell it in defiance of the excise man. All this was part of the game; the officials tried to be more watchful, but were always conscious that a point would ultimately be reached where it was simply not worthwhile to collect a little more revenue for a lot of trouble.

Indirect taxation had another advantage from the Government's point of view. The ultimate taxpayer – the consumer – often hardly noticed that he was being taxed. To critics of Government policy, the very ease of collection and the 'painlessness' of payment was a serious criticism of indirect taxation. The customs duties could easily become automatic and perpetual. Thus Parliament's control over taxation, which was the principal source of its power, might be eroded.

In the late seventeenth century, there was a lively argument about the relative morality of customs and excise duties. Customs duties fell mainly on the comfortably off; excise duties fell largely, though by no means exclusively, on the poor. Was it just to tax the poor? On one side, it might be urged that poor people, just like rich people, benefited from civil peace which the organs of government maintained and ought to pay for it. On the other side, it could be contended that the burden of a small tax on a poor man was far heavier than the burden of a much larger tax on a rich man – and so questions about the relative measure of sacrifice were stirred up.

There was also an active discussion about whether customs duties, and even to some extent excise duties as well, could be regarded as 'voluntary' taxation. A man might go through life without consuming any of the 'luxury' items which were liable to customs duties, and to that extent it was entirely his own choice whether to pay those duties or not.

Excise was a different matter, for it was almost impossible to avoid consuming some of the simple, home-produced items which were liable to duty; but even here a large measure of choice existed as to how much was to be consumed. In the seventeenth century, it was much safer to drink beer than to drink water; but many quite poor people undoubtedly elected to consume a good deal more beer than was essential for biological requirements. Much of that beer was brewed at home and did not attract the attention of the excise man; but a good deal was sold commercially, and poor people paid, indirectly, the duties which were levied upon it.

Whatever the general merits or demerits of indirect as opposed to direct taxes, few people denied that direct taxes were sometimes necessary as well. The system which was operated for the collection of the 'Assessed' taxes was efficient in the sense that the yield was more or less what it was supposed to be; but the manner of assessment was open to considerable objections. There was often a suspicion that the local assessors were distinctly partial in their treatment of individual taxpayers. Furthermore, some parts of the country were treated more favourably than others. These favoured places tended to be areas whose populations were over-represented in Parliament and which were thereby able to persuade the legislature to look kindly on their assessment.

The circumstances of the Restoration are relevant to an understanding of the immediate and practical financial problems which faced the new Parliament. Oliver Cromwell died in 1658. Thereafter, the system of government over which he had presided more or less fell to pieces. The Commonwealth perished, 'not with a bang but a whimper'. There were elections in the spring of 1660, and in May of that year it was Parliament itself which invited Charles to occupy the throne of his father. Available evidence suggests that the welcome which the King received was massive, unfeigned and well-nigh universal.

The 'Convention Parliament' – that is, the Parliament which summoned Charles II to the throne – contained a substantial number of people who had played a prominent part in the Cromwellian administration, and it was anxious to make a smooth transition from the old system to the new. The King for his part had no interest in revenge for its own sake, but had much interest in ensuring that the return from his 'travels' should be permanent.

Some important financial decisions had to be taken within a short time of the Restoration. The army which had been raised by the Cromwellians had to be paid off, for no government anywhere is stable in the presence of large numbers of unpaid and disaffected soldiers. Nearly £1 million was required for that purpose. It was also generally agreed that various ancient privileges of the Crown should be abolished and Parliament was prepared to pay the King £100,000 a year for surrendering them.

An estimate was made of Royal needs for the future, and these were set at £1.2 million a year. This sum covered the ordinary business of government, including military and naval needs, as well as the King's private requirements. Parliament agreed that this money should be provided. Such was the popular enthusiasm for a restored monarchy that it was possible to raise over £26,000 – a substantial sum in those days – as a 'free and voluntary present to His Majesty'.

Voluntary contributions, however, would clearly not suffice to meet revenue needs. The bulk of the regular revenue would be drawn from customs, which were supposed to produce £400,000, and excise, which was supposed to produce £250,000.[7] As an emergency measure, there was to be a Monthly Assessment of £70,000 for eleven months.

A 'poll tax' was also applied. This was archaic in form even by the standards of the time. Those in receipt of Poor Rate paid nothing; ordinary subjects paid 6d or 1 shilling (2.5p or 5p), after which there was a rising scale of payment, culminating in Dukes and Archbishops. What was being taxed, therefore, was not income, capital or land, but social status.

There was no question of repaying debts contracted by governments of the Commonwealth, but there were outstanding debts which had been owed by Charles I, while the new King's debts at the Restoration were set at £925,000; they reached nearly £3 million ten years later. The original intention had been to keep these sums separate from the annual payments, but in practice no special provisions were made. The King was usually able to raise substantial sums from time to time to meet shortfalls, drawing on such varied sources as his wife's dowry, the sale of Dunkirk and subventions from the King of France.[8]

At the turn of 1660–1, new House of Commons elections were held. The resulting 'Cavalier' or 'Pensioners' Parliament could be described as 'more royal than the King'. There is little indication, however, that the new Parliament took a radically different view of public finance from its predecessor.

Soon after the Restoration it became clear that there would be an annual shortfall of around £250,000 from the requirement of £1.2 million. How far this was the result of people not doing their sums properly and how far it was the result of the rather depressed state of the economy at the time does not seem entirely clear. Whatever the reason for the shortfall, further taxes were introduced to meet the problem.

At first the old 'subsidies' were revived, but these lasted for just a few years, when they were replaced by other kinds of taxation. Rather confusingly, the word 'subsidy' continued to be applied to new taxes of a different kind which were introduced from time to time. The 'Monthly Assessments' were brought back. These were still seen as essentially emergency taxes, to be levied in times of special need, and did not become a regular annual tax until after the 'Revolution' of 1688.[9]

Most famous of the new taxes was the Hearth Tax, or Chimney Tax, which was commenced in 1662, at the rate of 2 shillings (10p) on every hearth. This tax was particularly hated, and remained so until its abolition towards the end of the century. Although the very poorest people were exempt, the tax fell on a wide section, probably the large majority, of the total population, including people of very modest means. It was hard for sophists to argue, in the English climate, that domestic heating was a superfluous luxury.

Other taxes appeared from time to time, but tended to lapse when immediate needs abated. Thus, a spate of new taxes was introduced in 1670, including taxes on bankers; on land and tenements; on personal estates; and on income from public offices.

The balance between 'normal' taxes which were mainly indirect, and 'extraordinary' direct taxes, was more or less successful in Charles II's reign. A couple of wars with the Dutch imposed financial burdens which seemed heavy by the standards of the time, but by comparison with later wars appear very light. For the last decade of Charles's reign the country was at peace. This not only reduced the taxation needs, but it provided the further bonus that customs revenue was substantially enhanced as trade increased.

The mechanics of tax collection was still in the process of active evolution during the second part of the seventeenth century. At the time of the Restoration, there was not much of what might be called a civil service in the modern sense of the term. Nor was there any proper inventory of possible subjects of taxation, such as land, or incomes or the wealth possessed by individuals. This was part of the trouble with 'Assessments': even if people had really sought to make them work fairly, nobody had enough hard knowledge about the wealth, or the population, of different parts of the country.

For this reason, among others, the ancient device of tax-farming was used to collect taxes in the aftermath of the Restoration.[10] Individuals undertook the responsibility of collecting particular taxes, and those who controlled the Royal Treasury were not unduly worried what means were used to raise the money or how much personal profit the tax-farmers made from the transaction. The arrangement was useful to the Government, because tax-farmers could often be persuaded to pay substantial sums in advance of receipts for the privilege of appointment, thus bridging the gap between the decision to levy a tax and the point at which the money passed into Government hands. Tax-farming had the additional advantage that it provided a convenient way of compensating Royalists who had suffered heavy losses in the mid-century. In practice, this system produced such a poor yield for the Government that it was soon largely abandoned: for customs in 1671; for excise in 1683; and for the Hearth Tax in 1684.[11]

When tax-farming was abolished, full-time officials were appointed. By 1690, there were over 2,500 revenue officials, with approximately equal numbers allocated to customs and excise.[12] This new arrangement also had indirect advantages. It afforded infinite possibilities of patronage; and officials at all levels who owed their jobs to the Government could be regarded as reliable supporters, whatever troubles might beset it.

Public finance underwent other dramatic changes in the Restoration period. Money from taxation was often not available to the Treasury until some time after it had been granted by Parliament. This was one of several factors which encouraged the development of a banking system during the reign of Charles II – despite the dark suspicion that bankers were 'the Commonwealth's men'.

The developing banking system received a sharp check from the 'Stop of the Exchequer' of January 1671/2,[13] when repayment of, and interest on, Treasury orders were suspended. Such a move was practically an act of national bankruptcy and spread nationwide panic. It did considerable long-term damage of the financial credit of the Treasury and a substantial period elapsed before confidence was restored. For the time being, bankers responded to dubious credit in a predictable way – by demanding high interest.

Other changes which affected the Treasury during the latter part of the seventeenth century would later prove of immense importance, although the full implications of those changes would not become apparent for many years to come.

Immediately after the Restoration, the Treasury was controlled by the Privy Council and did not exercise any primacy among the great Departments of State.[14] In 1667, the Lord Treasurer, the Earl of Southampton, died. The King did not immediately appoint a successor, but established instead a Commission to perform the Treasurer's functions. Thereafter, Treasurers were appointed from time to time, but Commissions became equally common.

The new Commissioners (or Lords of the Treasury, as they were sometimes called) included several very able man, of whom Sir George Downing is the most famous, and soon began to claim enormous new powers. An Order in Council of 1667/8 laid down a substantial list of changes. Henceforth, for example, all revenue officers were to be appointed on Treasury recommendation; while money warrants for much government business had to be countersigned by the Commissioners. Sloppy financial practices were tightened up. Hitherto, tax-farmers had often passed the money they collected direct to Government creditors or officials;[15] under the new dispensation, all public finance passed through the Treasury. As a result, prospects of patronage through the Treasury exceeded those of any other Department.

The Treasury, however, was still considerably limited in its functions by the temporary nature of most direct taxation. A regular system of collection was evolving for customs, excise and the Hearth Tax; but collection of the 'Assessed' taxes, and other ephemeral taxes which were periodically dreamed up, ultimately depended on the diligence of influential local people, often JPs, who were sometimes reluctant to collect revenue from themselves and their friends.

In the second half of Charles II's reign, English Crown finances experienced a great improvement. Several factors were at work: better methods of tax collection following the demise of tax farming; a condition of peace after the end of the Third Dutch War in 1673/4; general improvements in trade and industry; perhaps the greater willingness of the wealthier classes to make the system work now that they had contrived to pass a substantial component of the tax burden on to the poor. Debts were paid off, and from 1673 the King was able to receive the full £1.2 million promised by Parliament at the Restoration.[16] It looked as though Parliament's strongest weapon in dealings with the King, the power of taxation, was beginning to buckle.

2 Revolution and After

In the 1670s, it became evident that Charles II would not have legitimate issue. The heir-presumptive was his brother James, Duke of York, whose Catholic sympathies were unconcealed. This fact caused considerable apprehension in some quarters and played a substantial part in the appearance of the Whig and Tory Parties. But when Charles died in February 1684/5, his brother became James II of England and VII of Scotland without immediate difficulties.

When he succeeded to the throne, James II/VII ordered his officials to continue collecting customs. This was a technical illegality, for customs had only been granted for his brother's lifetime; but it is difficult to see what else James could have done. He soon sought to legitimise the situation. Parliament had not met for a number of years, but James decided to summon a new one, and a General Election was called.

Thanks in part to some recent changes in Borough charters, the new Parliament was particularly docile. It ratified the King's earlier collection of customs and gave authority for their collection, along with excise and Hearth Tax, for the future. Other duties were imposed, bringing the Royal revenue to about £2 million a year:[1] a sum substantially greater than Charles II had enjoyed. As in the last few years of Charles's reign, there was no need to impose any further collection of the direct 'Assessed' taxes. Soon Parliament was dissolved and did not meet again in James's reign. Parliament was only required in order to authorise taxation and to make new statutes. If existing laws were satisfactory and revenue adequate, there was no need for a king to summon Parliament.

The record of James II/VII's short reign is mostly outside the present story. Despite earlier attempts to exclude him from the throne, the two revolts – one in England and one in Scotland – which were launched against him in 1685, the first year of his reign, were unsuccessful. The King's heir-presumptive was his daughter Mary, wife of the Protestant Dutch stadtholder William of Orange, leader of the continental alliance against Louis XIV of France.

But in June 1688, James's second wife produced a son. There was now a real possibility that James would be followed by a whole dynasty which was not only Catholic in religion, but was also capable of performing the business of government without Parliament's assistance.

Soon some of the Whig magnates sent a formal invitation to William of Orange, to come to England. In November and December 1688, his army moved towards London. The King's cause was badly managed and, before the end of the year, James had fled to France. Early in 1689, a Convention with dubious legal authority was summoned to face a complex constitutional crisis which admitted of various possible solutions.

William had been invited to Britain not primarily because of James's various inadequacies, or even because most of the aristocracy wanted a Protestant King rather than a Catholic King, but because the Whigs did not want a King at all in the traditional sense of the term, preferring a sort of Life President whom they could keep under firm control, most particularly in matters of finance. Soon the Convention drew up a Declaration of Rights, which expressed unambiguously the importance of Parliament in the new scheme of things.

On that clear understanding, the English throne, and soon the throne of Scotland as well, was offered to William and Mary jointly. Mary's *de jure* claim to the throne was not very good, but it was vastly better than that of her husband. Yet nobody doubted that he was the real sovereign, and her death in 1694 did not end William's reign. At the beginning, Ireland was away from William's reach and continued to recognise James; but in 1690 William was victorious at the Battle of the Boyne then in the following year at Aughrim, and resistance in Ireland soon collapsed.

Although State finances had been on an even keel while James was King, the new reign threw everything in doubt. At an early stage of his progress toward the throne, William had indicated his dislike for the Hearth Tax and soon the decision was taken to abolish it. This added substantially to the popularity of the new King and the régime which he came to serve; but it also increased the difficulty of achieving adequate revenue, for the hated tax was bringing in well over £200,000 a year by 1688.

Other sources of revenue which had been regular in the past now became more uncertain. When Parliament met early in the new reign, it was much more determined to bargain sharply with the new King than its predecessors had been in 1660 or 1685. William was Parliament's creature, and in the debates on public finance many MPs made it very clear that they did not propose to repeat the generosity – or laxity – which had been shown towards his two predecessors.[2]

A significant indication of the new approach was the policy towards 'tunnage and poundage' – the principal customs revenue. Hitherto, this had been granted at the beginning of a reign for the King's lifetime; now it was granted for just four years. An unfortunate Bishop received the task of explaining this decision to William. He employed the clever, but casuistic, argument that what worried Parliament was not the present sovereign, but his possible successors. Thus it was necessary to set a good precedent.

If the King accepted the arrangement he would be acclaimed not just by his own subjects, but by succeeding ages.[3] Whether William believed in the sincerity of this assurance or not, he had little alternative but to act as if he was satisfied.

Another innovation was the 'Civil List', in the original sense of the term. Parliament accepted the view that £600,000 a year should be reserved for the civil, as opposed to military, expenses of government, including such items as the salaries of judges, ambassadors and civil servants, and Crown pensioners.[4] Even this sum was not all at the free disposal of the King. Parliament intended to ensure that neither William nor any future sovereign could rule without frequent appeals for grants, which would henceforth be made conditional on whatever other demand Parliament might care to make.

William was more concerned with continental interests than with his father-in-law's kingdoms. Unlike his two predecessors, whose general policy had been to avoid war whenever possible, his overriding aim had long been to counter the aspirations of Louis XIV, and he had no objection to war as the means of so doing. One must suppose that the men who summoned him to the throne perceived the logical implications of that policy. By May 1689, three months after William became King, Britain was at war with France. Her allies were the Dutch and the Holy Roman Empire. The immediate conflict was to last a little more than eight years, but is commonly called the 'Nine Years War'. Britain remained on bad terms with France for much longer than that, and wars continued to be waged at intervals for a century and a quarter. Such was the price of the 'Glorious Revolution'.

If the first victim of war is always truth, the second is financial prudence. War acquires its own momentum, and warring states seldom ask themselves whether the conflict they have entered is worth the cost – even in money terms – which it necessarily demands. But the same preoccupation with conflict which prescribes that countries at war are usually prepared to go on prosecuting that war however exorbitant and ruinous the cost, also requires them to take a hard, cold look at their national finances to ensure that the money required for the war is levied in the most effective way. England in the 1690s was no exception to that rule.

The 'Nine Years War' of 1689–97 had an immediate effect on finances. Not only was it bound to prove expensive, like all wars, but it was also certain to impair customs receipts from the former trade with France. On top of this, a decision had already been taken, for practical purposes, to abolish the Hearth Tax. So the strain on other taxes was bound to be heavy.

Customs and excise duties were both periodically increased, and more kinds of goods came within the dutiable range. In James's reign, customs and excise had roughly balanced in the region of £600,000 a year. By the end of the Nine Years' War, both were closer to £1 million.

Direct taxes underwent a great change. A motley group of taxes came into being from time to time, but proved either short-lived, or with limited yield, or both. The 'Poll Tax' was applied on several occasions in the decade that followed the Revolution; but it was so widely hated by the poorer classes that it passed into disuse after 1698.

An imposition which proved much more durable was the House and Window Tax, which was introduced in 1696. The tax was originally introduced to pay for recoinage – but, like so many taxes, it lasted long after the original purpose had been discharged. The tax did not fall on cottages, but, above that level, houses were charged on a graduated scale according to number of windows. The object was very similar to that of the old Hearth Tax: to assess householders according to the size and grandeur of their properties; but the new tax was, if anything, even more objectionable than the old. Many properties exhibit to this day signs of devices which people employed to avert the tax and its later variations. These included blocked-up windows, and occasionally windows of curious shapes designed to illuminate more than one room and thus reduce the householder's liability.

From time to time at the end of the seventeenth century, other special taxes were imposed on a wide range of items, including stamped paper, hackney carriages, hawkers, births, deaths, marriages – and bachelors! – salt and tobacco pipes. Unlike the Window Tax, most of these taxes did not last long. One tax, however, proved both durable and important: the Stamp Duties, first imposed in 1694, which fell on various kinds of documents. In the first few years their yield was around £50,000 a year, but in 1698 additional duties were imposed and by the end of the century they were producing about £90,000.

'Monthly Assessments', which had not been required for most of the 1680s, were revived almost immediately William's reign began, in clear anticipation of war. Later in 1689, a different kind of 'Aid' was imposed. This time, there was an important difference of principle. Everybody was supposed to be taxed at the same rate, regardless of where they lived, instead of Parliament requiring a stated sum to be collected from each county.[5]

There was to be a charge on 'goods, wares, merchandizes or other chattels or personal estate' based on yearly profit; a charge on those holding 'any office or imployment of profit', save for military and naval officers; a charge on 'all lands tenements and hereditaments', and other similar charges. Assessment and collection of the tax was to be in the hands of Commissioners, who were required to be 'resident and having real estates to the value of one hundred pounds'[6] – effectively confining the duty to members of the landowning classes, whose services were unpaid.

As war had been joined by this time, this new 'Aid' was soon followed by others. The 1689 levy was at the rate of 1 shilling in the pound (5 per cent); it was followed by two levies, totalling 3 shillings, in 1690. A shilling of levy was reckoned to produce a revenue of almost exactly £500,000.

'Aids' of this kind were to remain the principal form of direct taxation for more than a century to come. They were not always levied at the same rate. At first, they were not demanded at regular intervals, like modern direct taxes. As need arose, an 'Aid' of 1, 2, 3 or 4 shillings in the pound would be required. It soon became clear, however, that the overall yield per shilling of the new tax was dropping. And so, in 1698, Parliament decided that in future it would use the valuation which had been imposed in 1692. That expedient was to remain in place for an astonishingly long time to come.

The 'Aid' was the most high-yielding of all taxes in the closing years of the seventeenth century. Taking William's reign as a whole (1689–1702), it produced about £19 million, against about £13 million each for customs and excise and about another £13 million for all other taxes.[7] It was also gradually changing in character. To appreciate what was happening, it is necessary to consider the manner of assessment and collection of the 'Aid'.

The Commissioners set up for each County or Borough were charged to deliver precepts on property owners. Assessors were appointed, who were required to determine the true value of the property and to charge accordingly. As oaths were taken very seriously indeed, statements about the value of assessments were not normally required to be on oath. In practice, personal property could easily be concealed, while landed estates could not be concealed. Thus, from the start, land assessments were made much more strictly than assessments of personal property.

As time went on, the disparity increased. The distinguished historian of taxation, Stephen Dowell, noted more than a century ago,[8] that as:

> tradesmen and others assessed in respect of their personalty died off, or departed from the particular district, the assessors charged their quota upon the land, adding it to the previous charge upon the landowners, so that the tax, which was intended to rest in the first instance upon goods and offices, the residue only being charged on the land ... gradually became, in effect, a tax upon land ...

Soon, the occasional 'Aids' became generally known in ordinary speech as the 'Land Tax'. The assessment fell upon the actual user, whether freeholder, copyholder or tenant. Where the user was a tenant, however, he was entitled to deduct the sum charged from his rent. The 'land' which was being taxed, however, was 'land' in the lawyer's sense of the word, not 'land' in the classical economist's sense; and from this difference much confusion was likely to spring. The landowner was being taxed on the improvements he had made, as well as the natural resources over which he claimed rights of ownership.

Nevertheless, a Parliament in which the landed interest dominated both Houses was consenting to tax itself heavily, however crude and unscientific its conception of 'land' might be. That paradox calls for an explanation. A kind of Civil Service had already been built up to collect customs and excise. But the task of creating a similar bureaucracy to deal with direct taxation, and to apply a sort of general tax on wealth as Parliament had intended, was beyond its administrative capacity, even when 'Aids' became frequent. The level of customs duties could not be increased too far, because either the trade would be so reduced that revenue would dry up, or else large-scale smuggling would take place, however draconian the laws to punish smugglers.

The only other way to obtain a really substantial source of increased revenue was to boost excise duties. Not much more could be squeezed out of the poor in this way; excise could only yield a lot more revenue if the burden fell mainly on the classes represented in Parliament. However little the parliamentarians and their voters like the 'Land Tax', they liked excise even less. The explanation is in part psychological rather than strictly financial. Excise was collected by government officials; while the landowning classes collected their own 'Land Tax.'

Thus William's war required the taxpayer to contribute more money in various ways. The incidence, and the amount, of traditional indirect taxes had been increased; a new Window Tax had been introduced which effectively replaced the old Hearth Tax; while the 'Aid' or 'Land Tax' had been applied with increasing frequency, so that it soon came to be regarded as a regular imposition. At the time of the 'Glorious Revolution,' the annual tax yield had been around £2 million; by 1696, the last full year of the war, it was over £4.8 million.

But a new expedient was also introduced to help pay for the war. Like people of later times who have engaged in wars, men of the period of William III decided to pass on much of the cost of those wars to people of succeeding generations.

The origin of what became known as the 'National Debt' may be traced long before William's time. Thus, an Act of 1665 which imposed an additional 'Aid' had authorised loans to be raised on security of the proposed tax yield; while an Act of 1685 which imposed new customs duties had authorised loans on a similar basis.[9]

Measures like these, however, tied the loan to a particular tax. In the reign of William III, a new principle was introduced. Should one tax provide an inadequate yield, the loan could be serviced or extinguished from a different tax. This gave the investor much better security and was an important step towards the modern practice of consolidating public funds.

There was an even more important difference between the new loans and the old ones. Loans which had been raised in earlier times had been short-term in character. In the 1690s, long-term loans began to be raised, to bridge the gap between taxation yields and Government requirements. Some of these loans involved a combination of investment and gambling. The first lottery loan was issued in 1694 and was soon followed by others. Subscribers were entitled to interest and also participated in a draw for money prizes. Another device was the tontine, by which people paid for an annuity, the benefits for survivors becoming greater as other subscribers died. The debt on the new loans continued for a very long time. The last survivor of the tontine system, for example, lived until 1783, still receiving interest on a seventeenth-century debt.[10]

In 1688, there had been virtually no National Debt which required to be serviced; by the end of the Nine Years' War in 1697, the debt stood at around £16.7 million. Even at this early date, a substantial proportion of the National Debt – about 20 per cent in 1697 – was 'funded' – that is, it had been made part of a permanent State debt, with provision for payment of interest at a fixed rate. As time went on, an increasing part of the debt was 'funded'. In 1711, the 'funded' debt exceeded the 'unfunded' for the first time; from 1725 onwards the 'funded' element of the National Debt nearly always exceeded the 'unfunded' by a factor of ten or more.

A major new institution, the Bank of England, was set up in 1694, with special responsibility for management of the National Debt. Interest on this debt alone amounted to more than half of what had been the total Government revenue ten years earlier. In general terms, however, it was still accepted by all concerned that the bulk of the debt was of a 'temporary' character, and in the five years of peace which followed it was reduced to £14.1 million.

A series of events at the turn of the eighteenth century, mainly of a dynastic character, initiated a new war, usually called the War of the Spanish Succession. The English, the Dutch and the Holy Roman Empire again found themselves in alliance against France. Fighting had already begun when, in March 1702, William III died and was succeeded by his wife's sister Anne; but a few more weeks would elapse before war was formally declared.

The new war lasted even longer than William's war and continued for nearly the whole of Anne's reign. It is generally remembered in Britain for the bloody victories of Marlborough; but it is also linked with a further quantum leap in burdens sustained by the taxpayer. A recent author has calculated that military expenditure amounted to about 66 per cent of total government spending during the period 1702–13.[11] Average annual expenditure, which had been £2 million in 1688, and £5.5 million during the Nine Years War, shot up to £7 million in the War of the Spanish Succession.[12]

The general trend of taxation was upwards, whether in peace or war. Customs yields fluctuated according to the extent to which trade was possible in wartime conditions; but from 1697 onwards they were never below £1 million, and sometimes over £1.5 million. Excise duties followed a rather similar pattern and by the end of the war in 1712 were over £1.8 million. For most of the war, yields of the so-called 'Land Tax', with the other much smaller direct taxes, hovered around £2 million.

The expedient of raising a large part of wartime expenditure through additions to the National Debt was again followed in the new war. In the 11 years 1702–12 inclusive, the mean annual spending was £7.76 million, while the mean annual borrowing was £2.45 million, or 31.5 per cent of the total.[13]

A matter which would have considerable bearing on future taxation was the question of union between England and Scotland. Anne was acknowledged as sovereign of both Kingdoms; but a large question hung on the succession thereafter. She had had numerous children, but all were dead before she became Queen in 1702. It was by no means self-evident that the same individual would succeed Anne to the two Thrones. In 1701, the English had decided that succession would pass to the descendants of Sophia of Hanover. The Scottish Parliament had reserved its rights on the matter, and it was not unlikely that it would prefer the son of James VII of Scots and II of England.

The recent history of Scotland had been markedly different from that of England in various ways, and some aspects of that history underlined the uncertainty about even a tenuous union persisting between the two countries. Scotland was a much poorer country than England. Scottish Crown revenues – including those that derived from Royal estates – were of small value. A measure of 1663 gave the King the right to tax imports, but Scottish foreign trade was not very extensive at this time. There were other more dramatic marks of Scotland's poverty. In the closing years of the seventeenth century, famine and associated diseases wiped out nearly a quarter of the country's population.[14] The Darien Scheme of colonisation in central America had attracted heavy investment from the Scottish middle classes, but had been sabotaged by the politicking of William II of Scots and III of England. The Scots had plenty of other reasons for loathing the Dutchman whom the English aristocracy had foisted upon them.

The choice which both Kingdoms faced was either to establish a much closer union than the century-old union of the Crowns, or else to separate completely. The English parliamentarians, who were concerned with a possible military threat from the north, and also many Scots, who hoped to be free from the trade barriers which the English currently imposed against them, preferred union. In the end, large-scale bribery of Scottish parliamentarians decided the matter. Terms of union were agreed by the Parliaments of the two countries, and in 1707 this union took effect. The Scottish Parliament was suppressed, and the new Parliament of Great Britain included Scotish members in both Houses. The establishment of the Scottish Kirk, and of the Scottish Courts, was preserved.

The Union included a number of financial terms. After a transitional period, there would be complete economic union. A lump sum just short of £400,000, known as the 'equivalent', was granted to Scotland to meet her future liabilities on the English National Debt. English customs duties and most of the excise duties would apply in Scotland; but Scotland would be exempt from certain English taxes, notably the Stamp Duties and the House and Window Taxes. The 'Land Tax' was applied, but with the special provision that Scotland's liability would be set at £48,000 as against England's assessment at almost £2 million when the rate stood at 4 shillings in the pound, with reductions *pro rata* when the English rate was lower. This 40-fold difference recognised the dire poverty of Scotland.

3 Eighteenth-Century Taxation

> Governments are always without any exception the greatest spendthrifts of society.
>
> Adam Smith, Wealth of Nations bk. 2, ch. 3

Anne died in 1714. In the 26 years which had followed the expulsion of her father, many great changes in public finance had taken place. The finances of Scotland had been amalgamated with those of England. Not only customs and excise but also the 'Land Tax', had become, in most people's minds, a permanent feature of the taxation system. The Hearth Tax had disappeared, but something remarkably like it had been restored in a more durable form as the House and Window Tax. A regular National Debt had come into existence, and the interest on that debt alone was costing the taxpayer over £3 million a year – 50 per cent more than the total tax bill had been in 1688. Future governments would always need to reckon interest on the National Debt as a major item in their budgeting requirements. The annual taxation revenue, which had been around £2 million in 1688, had stood at over £5 million for a full decade and would never again fall below that figure.

Most of these changes are attributable, directly or indirectly, to the wars of William and Anne. The pattern of taxation in the period which followed Anne's death is linked in an intricate manner with matters ranging from public finance to dynastic succession, from domestic politics to foreign policy and overseas wars.

Anne was succeeded by George, Elector of Hanover. The change of dynasty produced a great shift in political power. George had neither the wish nor the linguistic skill to preside over the meetings of Ministers, as his predecessors had done. One of George I's first acts as King, however, had been to dismiss the Lord Treasurer whom Anne had appointed just before her death, and thereafter the post was never restored. Effective power, not only over finance but over most kinds of State business, passed increasingly to the First Lord of the Treasury.

The law of the time required a General Election to be held shortly after the accession of a new sovereign. Party labels already existed, although consistent ideological distinctions between parties would be hard to discover. The new elections yielded a substantial majority to the Whigs, who were to remain in control for nearly half a century.

Figure 2   This is an early example of a cartoon of an essentially modern kind. Like other eighteenth-centruy cartoons, however, it was sold by itself at a price which would have been beyond the reach of most working people, and did not appear as an illustration to a magazine or newspaper. It was accompanied with a piece of doggerel, beginning 'See this dragon Excise / Has ten thousand eyes ...'

The cartoon refers to the 'Excise Crisis' of 1733. Sir Robert Walpole, later Earl of Orford, 'the first Prime Minister', was seeking to abolish the 'Land Tax' and replace it by an extended system of excise duties. This plan produced much protest, and was eventually abandoned.

Various heads of the dragon Excise are swallowing items which carried excise duties, while one head vomits a cascade of coins into the lap of Walpole. It was generally known that Walpole was amassing a huge fortune from his office, and this cartoon was particularly near the knuckle. Hawkers of the cartoon were arrested for seditious libel, but were discharged by the Court. Cartoonists and vendors of cartoons became practically immune from prosecution, and satirical drawings of this kind became common.

The year 1715 witnessed other great events. Most famous of these is the 'Fifteen', a major Scottish rising in favour of the 'Jacobite' claimant to the throne, James Edward Stuart, son of the exiled James VII of Scots and II of England. The 'Fifteen' was managed incompetently and was soon suppressed. The expense of so doing, however, was considerable, and in the following year the 'Land Tax' was increased briefly to defray the cost.

Within a few months of George's accession, the post of First Lord of the Treasury passed to Robert, later Sir Robert, Walpole. His first period in office would prove brief, but his attention was soon directed to the very large burden which the National Debt imposed upon the taxpayer. In 1714, the debt stood at £36.2 million and the interest stood at £3.02 million: an annual rate substantially over 8 per cent.[1] Service of the debt represented well over half of the annual State expenditure.

Walpole tackled the problem at two levels. He sought to reduce the high interest rates, which were related closely to the dubious creditworthiness of the State and its sources of revenue. He also took steps towards a reduction in the capital sum of the National Debt, with a view, perhaps, to eventual abolition. With that purpose in mind, a 'Sinking Fund' was created. This meant in practice that taxation would remain at a higher level than current expenditure demanded, in order gradually to pay off the debt.

Not long afterwards, Walpole was removed from office and any immediate schemes for retrenchment were vitiated by a new war – this time with Spain (1718–21). In 1721, however, he again became both First Lord of the Treasury and Chancellor of the Exchequer, and was to retain both offices for no less than 21 years. During this period, he acquired enormous authority and influence, and towards the end of his rule the term 'Prime Minister' was applied to him by his critics.

Walpole's 'reign' had an enormous effect on the course of events in several different fields, and in some areas this effect has persisted right down to the present day. Walpole was personally corrupt: the one Prime Minister to leave office very much more wealthy than he entered it; and he presided over a system of corruption affecting every facet of national life.

Yet Walpole's career had other features of a more attractive kind. He had the good sense to see that wars, whether victorious or not, usually cost vastly more – even in strict money terms – than any benefit they produce and set his face against unnecessary conflicts. The wars of William III and Anne had brought the National Debt into existence and had increased other burdens on the taxpayer as well. If taxation was to be reduced, peace was essential. There would then be a fair chance of winning tacit support of the nation for both the Government and the dynasty. For a long time Walpole successfully avoided repeating the errors that politicians had made in William's reign by involving themselves in the sovereign's continental interests.

This pacific policy enabled Walpole to make substantial incursions into the tax burden imposed by the National Debt. The capital sum of the debt was reduced to some extent: from £54.9 million in 1721 to £46.9 million in 1739; but the prospect of wiping out the debt altogether, which had seemed realistic in 1714, was really outside the range of practicality by the late 1730s. Walpole was more successful in producing a marked reduction in the annual interest burden falling on the taxpayer. Over the same period, this dropped from £3.3 million to just over £2 million.

Yet the general burden of taxation remained fairly stable during Walople's period of office, hovering around £6 million a year for most of the time. Overall customs revenues fluctuated from year to year, but the yield did not change much in the long term. They produced £1.45 million in 1721, £1.43 million in 1741. There was, however, a substantial shift in the incidence of customs duties. In particular, Walpole secured the removal of duties on exportation of manufactured goods, which were perceived as damaging to domestic producers. Customs duties were coming gradually to be seen not just as a means of raising revenue, but as an instrument of national economic policy.

Walpole favoured a general reduction in the 'Land Tax'. His thinking on the matter is indicated by a complaining letter in which he noted that 'the Land Tax falls on 400,000 men out of 8 million'.[2] For most of Walpole's tenure of office, the 'Land Tax' stood at 2 shillings in the pound. It rose to 3 shillings in the late 1720s, at a time when there appeared a serious risk of war, but it was soon returned to 2 shillings, and in 1731 was brought down to 1 shilling.[3] Walpole probably hoped eventually to remove the tax entirely. Success for this policy, however, turned not only on avoidance of war, but also on a certain willingness to increase excise.

Excise was widely regarded with immense suspicion. The poor, who were little affected by the 'Land Tax' and not much by customs duties, were bound to dislike it. Wealthier people disliked it too, largely because of its allegedly inquisitorial character. There was a lurking fear, eagerly fostered by his political opponents, that Walpole sought a 'general excise': the condition, one might say, which has been brought about in the twentieth century through the operation first of Purchase Tax and later of VAT.

Matters came to a head in 1733. Several issues were bound up together. Much argument took place over the seemingly innocuous proposal to transfer duties on wine and tobacco from customs – where they were widely evaded or avoided – to excise. More important, really, was the public debate over the Salt Tax. At a time when winter fodder was available in limited quantities only, many beasts were slaughtered in the autumn and salted down for consumption during the winter. A tax on salt would be borne by people of all classes, but it would inevitably fall hardest on the poor. There was also an argument for the view that the result of a tax on such a necessary commodity would be pressure for higher wages, which would raise costs of production and therefore damage all kinds of manufacture. As recently as 1730, the old Salt Tax had been abolished; but in 1733 the Government proposed to restore it, and simultaneously cut the 'Land Tax'.[4]

Fear of a 'General Excise' was not the only factor which induced many members of the landowning class to view with mixed feelings the prospect that the 'Land Tax' would shortly be reduced, and perhaps eventually abolished. In a few years, some emergency would be likely to arise which would make revival of the 'Land Tax' necessary. If that happened, Parliament would be unlikely to return to the 1692 valuation, which had been lopsided from the start and which, 40 years on, was palpably out of date. A new valuation would mean that some areas and some individuals would pay more. No doubt others would pay less; but, in matters of taxation, people who are likely to lose from a change will usually make much more noise than people who are likely to gain.

Other considerations disposed many politicians to resist Walpole's excise proposals. Tories, whether Jacobite or Hanoverian in their sympathies. had little hope of preferment while Walpole reigned supreme. By 1733, there were also many Whigs who, for some reason or other, had fallen foul of Walpole, who also wished to bring him down.

So a coalition of interests emerged. Amid scenes of great public excitement, Parliament threw out the Government's excise proposals,[5] although Walpole remained in office.

A remarkable example of a new kind of tax appeared in the Walpole period: a tax whose primary purpose was not financial but social. In the early eighteenth century, sales of gin among the London poor were enormous and the effects were visibly damaging both to the consumers' health and to public order. In 1729 an Act was passed, designed to impose a duty on gin and to require retailers to pay a substantial licence fee. The law was evaded, but a new and more effective 'Gin Act' was passed in 1736.[6] This measure also ran into trouble; but the principle that taxation might occasionally be applied 'to protect people from themselves' would prove of great importance in the future.

In 1739, Walpole's peaceful foreign policy broke at last and he was driven by colleagues into war – initially with Spain, but later with France as well. There were too many factors at work in favour of war: the continental interests of the King, the jingoistic 'patriotism' of men like the elder William Pitt, and the hopes of many people in the City of London that they could gain wealth from plunder. That conflict was to last until 1748. At the beginning of the war, Walpole made the accurate and punning observation, 'They now ring the bells, but they will soon wring their hands.'

It would have been better for Walpole's later reputation if he had left office when the war commenced. Instead, he remained at the helm for nearly three years, eventually departing in 1742. Succeeding Ministers were saddled with the war and they could not escape its financial implications.

After Walpole's fall in 1742, there was a good deal of tax juggling, but in one direction an important and durable change was made. It appeared at first sight little more than tinkering with an existing tax. The Window Tax was altered by setting a duty on all houses, while those with 20 windows or more were charged a further shilling for each window. One author has seen the modified House and Window Tax as 'the first tax aimed at property by taking an article of expenditure as *prima facie* evidence of the possession of means'.[7] This may be something of an overstatement, but there were serious problems in operating all existing taxes, and many people were disposed to seek a different basis of taxation.

By 1748, when the 'War of the Austrian Succession' at last ended in a compromise peace, the National Debt had increased much further: £46.9 million in 1739, £76.1 million in 1748. The greater security of investment, however, ensured that interest rates continued to decline, and the extra annual burden of around £800,000 which fell on the taxpayer was considerably less than the rising debt would have suggested. The idea of eventually paying off the debt through use of the Sinking Fund was again raised, but was rejected. By this date, the people who were paying for interest on the debt in their capacity as taxpayers were largely the very people who were receiving interest in their capacity as investors. So the attitude of the political classes towards the National Debt was becoming ambivalent.

The decline in interest rates on the National Debt must also have stirred conflicting sentiments. As has been seen, the rate in 1714 was over 8 per cent. By 1721 it was around 6 per cent. In 1749, a debt of £77.8 million required a charge of £2.981 million, a mean value of just over 3.8 per cent. Wise investors reflected, however, that this decline in investment returns was the mark of increased security.

In that year, 1749, Pelham was able to propose that 4 per cent stocks should be reduced to 3.5 per cent and – after seven years – to 3 per cent. He had difficulties in carrying the proposal, but eventually succeeded. Many government loans were consolidated at 3 per cent – the original 'consols' – and these were soon selling at well above par.[8] The annual debt charge, which hovered at around £3 million at the time of George I's accession in 1714, was roughly the same when his great-grandson George III came to the throne in 1760, while the National Debt stood at more than two and a half times the earlier figure. Means had thus been found by which large sums of money could be raised by a government more or less as required, and at low interest rates. Paradoxically, the policy of financial stability, which Walpole had linked so closely with the preservation of peace, now became the means by which it was possible for his successors to raise larger and larger sums of money for wars.

Other changes of taxation were taking place. Customs receipts tended, naturally enough, to rise in peacetime and decline in war, while the incidence of customs was changed considerably; but their yield did not change much overall. In 1714, they produced £1.6 million; in 1756, the sum was £1.8 million.

Excise receipts changed much more. In 1714 they stood at just over £2 million; by 1756 they were £3.6 million. Perhaps there was some substance in the fear of a 'General Excise' which had been expressed so pungently by Walpole's critics in 1733. The proportion of taxation revenue deriving from excise was also gradually creeping up: around 35 per cent at the death of Anne in 1714, about 45 per cent or 50 per cent in the middle 1750s.

The 'Land Tax' followed closely the cycle of peace and war. For most of his generally peaceful 'reign', Walpole kept it down to 2 shillings in the pound (10 per cent), and for a short time was able to reduce it to 1 shilling. When he was forced into war in 1739, it was brought to 4 shillings. When peace returned, it was again reduced: to 3 shillings in 1750, 2 shillings in 1753.

Yet there was an effective ceiling to the yield of the 'Land Tax'. A tacit assumption prevailed that it must never exceed 4 shillings in the pound. Thus as other taxes increased, so did the proportion claimed by the 'Land Tax' decline in a gradual, though irregular, manner.

In 1756, the 'Seven Years' War' broke out between Britain and France. The rising force in politics was the elder William Pitt, later Earl of Chatham. Effectively, Pitt controlled the war, while others – usually the Duke of Newcastle – attended to the business of underpinning the war politically and financially. Effectively, Pitt's overriding concern was not conquest for its own sake, but control of trade; and he had the enthusiastic backing of the most powerful interests in the City of London.

In 1760, when the war was in full spate, George II died and was succeeded by his grandson, George III. The new king was less than enthusiastic for the war and worked for the restoration of peace. In this matter George had the strong assistance of his former mentor, the Earl of Bute. Eventually the Newcastle–Pitt ministry was dismissed and Bute became First Lord of the Treasury.

Bute was widely unpopular with contemporaries and has generally been considered a failure by later historians. Yet in one respect he was remarkably successful. By the end of 1762 preliminaries of peace had been signed and the war was formally concluded in the following year.

The 'Seven Years War', as it became known, produced its notable victories, and by the time it was over Britain was visibly the dominant European Power both in North America and in India. The war also involved expenditure on a scale greatly exceeding that of previous conflicts. Military spending has been estimated at over £82 million, or 71 per cent of total government expenditure in the period.[9] Taxes rose. Annual taxation receipts, which had been around £7 million when the war began, were close to £10 million at the end. Customs duties rose by about £500,000, excise duties and the 'Land Tax' each by around £1 million, while there was a considerable spate of new taxes. As was becoming habitual in times of war, the Government allowed the National Debt to increase greatly. In 1756 this stood at £74.6 million, in 1763 it was £132.6 million. The annual interest on the debt, which had stood at £2.7 million in 1756, was almost £4.7 million at the end of the war.

Although the elder Pitt was disposed to believe that Britain could have achieved even more spectacular acquisition from the Seven Years War, her position in North America appeared superficially to have been strengthened enormously. British colonists were now free from any threat from the French. There was no longer a great stretch of French territory extending northwards from the Gulf of Mexico through the Alleghany Mountains to far beyond the St Lawrence, impeding westward expansion. Should not the colonists pay something for the immense benefits which they had recently secured as a result of the military and financial effort involved?

One of the many paradoxes of war is that the victors as well as the vanquished often finish up losing things for which they originally took up arms. Since the beginning of the eighteenth century, the white population of British North America had multiplied tenfold, and currently stood at around two million. The colonies had their own legislatures. One modern American writer has noted that

> each colony relied on a different mixture of poll, property and commerce taxes. By 1763 no two colonies had exactly the same revenue law ... Throughout the American colonies, tax laws overburdened the politically impotent and favored the politically powerful and the wealthy ...[10]

It was generally accepted in England, and seldom – if at all – confuted in America, that Britain had the right to 'regulate trade' of the colonies.

The various Navigation Acts had long given effect to that doctrine. The colonists were not permitted to import European goods, with the exception of salt, save in British or colonial ships.[11] This was part of a much wider economic system, often called mercantilism. Mercantilist doctrine prescribed, among other things, that colonial possessions exist for the benefit of the mother country in order to supply raw materials and receive manufactured goods. Smuggling, however, was so extensive in the colonies that mercantilism did not impose a heavy burden on the Americans.

If the British Government had been willing to wink at constant evasions of the law by American colonists, all might have been well; but, in the immediate aftermath of the Seven Years War there was a general feeling in Britain that massive wartime expenditure must be followed by serious retrenchment and by much more rigorous attitudes towards the colonists. Belief in mercantilist theory was one thing; enforcement of that theory in practice was very different.

The root of the American revolution lay not in the obstinacy of the King, but in Parliament's insistence on exercising powers of taxation which hitherto had existed mainly in theory. In 1764, Revenue Acts were passed by the British Parliament imposing customs duties on certain luxury goods entering America from British or European sources. This led to a general American boycott of those goods, but it hardly contravened established views, either in Britain or in America, as to what Parliament could legitimately do if it so desired.

In the following year, 1765, however, a real innovation appeared: the Stamp Act, associated with George Grenville, First Lord of the Treasury. The Stamp Act, 'the first internal tax to be imposed by the British Parliament upon the colonies',[12] imposed considerable duties on American legal documents and also on newspapers – which were regarded as a luxury in those days. To make matters much worse, cases of contravention of the Stamp Acts were to be tried in the Admiralty Court, without a jury. An American jury would be most unlikely to convict in such a case; while an Admiralty judge sitting alone was much more likely to do so.

The Stamp Acts were a disastrous failure. There was a good deal of violence in America. Within a year, the Act was repealed, to the great delight of many British as well as American politicians. The Americans, however, had fired a shot across the bows of the British Government, providing plain warning that American patience was not unlimited.

The next phase of the American saga concerned a new spate of indirect taxes. In 1767, Charles Townshend, British Chancellor of the Exchequer, introduced new duties on various items, including tea. The underlying thinking appears to have been the view that these would go some way towards providing a tax compensation for a reduction in the British 'Land Tax' from 4 to 3 shillings in the pound.

Again, what worried the colonists was not the existence of an Act of Parliament which imposed duties, but the plain intention of the British Government to enforce them. There were loud protests from the colonies, and in 1770 most of the duties were repealed. Tea, however, was the exception, and a profitable trade in smuggling tea persisted.

What sparked off real trouble in America was not over-burdensome taxation, but a mortal threat to the smuggling industry. The British foothold in India was growing, through the commercial and military operations of the chartered East India Company. The Company had the ear of the British Government; and it also had vast surplus stores of tea. Strict mercantilism prescribed that this tea, when destined for America, should be taken first to British ports; but the old rules were formally relaxed and in 1772 direct trade between India and America was permitted. Tea thus provided would have been so cheap in America that smuggling would have been undercut by lawful trade. The Americans – or at least their vociferous publicists – declared that this was a British stratagem designed to trick them into paying the Townshend duties.

There followed the 'Boston Tea Party' of 1773, when loads of tea were tipped into the harbour by colonists disguised as Amerindians. The British reacted by closing the port of Boston and revoking the Charter of Massachusetts. Thereafter, events slid rapidly towards war between Britain and the colonists. The high-sounding call for 'no taxation without representation' was raised on the American side; but nobody had ever devised a convincing plan for 'representing' the American colonies and so in practice the slogan meant 'no taxation at all'.

The first true engagement between the British and the colonials was fought at Lexington in April 1775. After considerable doubts and hesitation, the American colonies formally declared independence in July of the following year. Thereafter the conflict escalated, eventually involving France, Spain and the Netherlands on the colonists' side. Peace was concluded in 1783, with formal acknowledgement of the colonists' independence.

The American War of Independence was, from the British point of view, a complete disaster. It ended in defeat and it cost a great deal of money. Just how much it cost is not easy to say. A possible way of quantifying the cost is to say that the annual expenditure on navy, army and ordnance together was running at around £3.8 or £3.9 million in 1774 and 1775, while during the period 1776–83 inclusive it totalled over £105 million, corresponding with an extra cost of about £80 million. This does not complete the tally, for the international instability caused by the war made higher 'defence' spending necessary thereafter.

The sort of taxation with which people were familiar in the eighteenth century was not very elastic. Existing customs duties could not be increased much without making smuggling even more attractive; while international trade necessarily fell as a result of war and thus tended to reduce the yield. The annual yield of customs during the war was in the range £2.3 to £3 million, which is roughly what it had been for the previous decade.

The 'Land Tax' stood at 3 shillings in the pound at the outbreak of war. It was promptly raised to 4 shillings, and remained at that rate until the whole system of direct taxation was radically revised by the younger Pitt at the end of the century. The addition brought in the predicted extra £500,000 a year.

As the war proceeded, new, or additional, taxes were devised from time to time. An Inhabited House Tax, related to the value of the house, was introduced as an addition to the old House and Window Tax. Stamp Duties were increased, and taxes were imposed on legacies. Familiar targets of taxation such as salt, sugar, soap and beer attracted further attention. So did unfamiliar items like male servants, fire insurance and property sold at auctions. These, and many other new or increased taxes, brought new burdens on the taxpayer and added to the unpopularity of the Prime Minister, Lord North; but all of them together could not radically alter the fiscal situation.

So current taxation could only go a small way towards paying for the American war, whose futility was becoming increasingly apparent. In 1775, the annual State taxation revenue stood at around £11 million; over the period 1776–83 it averaged a little over £12 million. The only device remaining for the Government was to increase the National Debt. This took place on an enormous scale. The debt in 1775 was £127 million; by 1783 it stood at £231 million. Over the same period the annual charge rose from £4.7 million to £8.0 million. The old expedient of forcing future generations of taxpayers to pay for current wars was applied yet again.

Not long after the formal conclusion of peace in 1783, a new appointment was made to the two posts of First Lord of the Treasury and Chancellor of the Exchequer: the 24-year-old William Pitt the younger, second son of the Earl of Chatham: the one man in British history who was to spend most of his adult life in the highest political office of all.

Pitt started off with many advanced ideas. He favoured reform of the bizarre electoral system. He was an opponent of the slave trade. His commercial treaty with France in 1786 ended the 'customs war' between the two countries. In so far as he could, Pitt 'rationalised' taxation. Thus, customs and excise duties were brought into the Consolidated Fund in 1787.

Pitt had read that great economic work, Adam Smith's *Wealth of Nations*, which was first published in 1776. Adam Smith was to exert an enormous influence on economic thinking, from his own time down to the present. His support for Free Trade was constantly invoked, most particularly in the nineteenth and twentieth centuries, but his four 'maxims of taxation' are equally relevant in the present context. These maxims were frequently invoked in support or in criticism of fiscal policies and they do appear to have exerted a real influence on taxation practice.

Smith's first maxim was that taxation should be 'equal or equitable' – that taxpayers 'ought to contribute to the support of the government... in proportion to the revenues which they respectively enjoy'. His second maxim was that taxation should be 'certain and not arbitrary', his third that it should be 'convenient as to the time and manner of the levy'. Smith's fourth maxim was that tax should be 'economical... not too expensive to collect and not unduly obstructive and discouraging to the taxpayer'. Both the first and the fourth of these maxims led him to the view – which Pitt warmly endorsed – that taxes on the poor were not only burdensome to the weakest members of society, but also an impediment to trade, for they would necessarily lead to demands for higher wages, which would raise costs of production.

The results of a prolonged period of peace, and the skilled control of an able finance minister in the period from Pitt's accession to power down to 1792, were substantial. The annual Government revenue had increased by nearly 50 per cent: £12.7 million in 1783, £18.6 million in 1792. To a considerable extent, this increase may be attributed to rising productivity, now that the 'industrial revolution' was beginning to gather pace. Customs produced £1 million or so – what might today be called a 'peace bonus' – while excise yielded well over £3 million more. In the first few years of Pitt's ministry the National Debt rose a little; but ever since 1786 it had been dropping marginally year by year.

Government expenditure was a little below taxation revenue. In 1792, the total figure was just under £17 million. Of this sum, £9.3 million was required for debt charges, £5.6 million for 'defence'. The cost of everything else put together was around £2 million. Unless he could find some way of drastically reducing the National Debt, there was not much that Pitt, or anybody else, could do to bring down the total sum of taxation very much. Nobody anticipated that in the next few years taxation and the Debt alike would soar to figures completely without precedent.

4 The French Wars and After

> The system of raising funds necessary for wars by loan practices whole-sale, systematic and continual deception on the people. The people do not really know what they are doing. The consequences are adjourned into a far future.
>
> W.E. Gladstone. Parl. Deb. 1854 cxxii 1413–79

For some time after the French Revolution began in 1789, the British Government and British taxation were little affected, although there was a good deal of speculation about what the implications of the Revolution might be for Britain. As that Revolution became increasingly violent and bloody, concern began to grow.

The execution of Louis XVI in January 1793 produced a widespread reaction of horror. Less than a fortnight later war broke out between Britain and the French republic. The new conflict would prove by far the longest in which Britain had been involved for centuries, and by far the costliest to date. Public spending would increase to an unprecedented extent, and new ideas about taxation would be introduced which would have enormous repercussions right down to our own day.

The massive increase in expenditure between the Restoration and the beginning of the French Wars had nothing to do with any change in the perceived functions of government. The sums granted for the monarch's personal requirements, for the cost of the diplomatic service, for the administration of justice, and so on – all these sums increased, but not to a degree which would exert a major effect on overall State expenditure. The growing bulk of taxation was, overwhelmingly, money paid for war: money to defray the cost of current wars, money to prepare for future wars or money to service debts incurred in past wars. Some of the eighteenth-century wars resulted in victory, one in defeat, and at least one in what might be called a draw. All, without exception, resulted in a permanent increase in burdens upon the taxpayer.

When war was entered again in 1793, it was at once seen to be an incomparably more crucial struggle than any in which Britain had been engaged for a very long time indeed. Pitt, in his dual capacity of First Lord of the Treasury and Chancellor of the Exchequer, took the lead in attempting to raise the money required. As in earlier wars, financial prudence went to the winds; but this time the effect was much more spectacular.

Ever since 1787, Pitt had contrived to keep annual expenditure a little below income, which had permitted a very gradual reduction of the

34

National Debt. In 1793, the position was reversed, but not to a great extent: £19.6 million expenditure, £18.1 million receipts. In the next few years, enormous sums were required for the armed forces and for bribing Britain's continental allies to continue fighting. The gap between income and expenditure widened enormously, so that by 1797 an expenditure of £57.7 million was met by only £21.4 million income: a gap of £36.3 million. From the beginning of the war until 1797, the National Debt had risen by the incredible sum of over £110 million. This was not exclusively a problem for people of the future; the interest had to be funded year by year. The annual charge, which had been £9.3 million in 1792, was almost £13.6 million in 1797.

Pitt had been making upward adjustments of taxation during the intervening period – on wine, spirits, tea, sugar, tobacco, bricks and various other items. But by 1797, the very solvency of the State was in doubt. The value of government 'consols', which stood roughly at par in 1792, was down to 55 in January 1797, and plummeted further in the late winter and spring.[1] Cash payments at the Bank of England were suspended and they were not resumed for 22 years. War or no war, the Government was compelled to reduce its spending, which was down to £47.8 million in 1798. At the same time, a radically new view of taxation was being forced on the Government.

In 1798, there were several taxation changes, two of which would prove of great importance. The first concerned what were known as the 'Assessed Taxes'. This was a miscellaneous group of taxes, falling mainly on the well-to-do, and included such items as taxes on houses, carriages, men servants and horses which were used for 'luxury', purposes like riding, racing or drawing carriages. The 'Assessed Taxes' had been lumped together in 1785 for administrative purposes. At the time, this change had not affected the taxpayer.

In 1798, however, the 'Assessed Taxes' were multiplied by a factor ranging from three at the bottom end of the scale to five at the top. There was, however, a proviso that nobody was to be taxed under this head at a sum which would exceed a certain proportion of his income. For incomes over £200 a year the figure was set at 10 per cent; for lower incomes it was set at a lower figure. A person claiming that this sum would be exceeded under the new 'Triple Assessment' was authorised to render a statement of his total income, and the tax would then abate in so far as it exceeded the stated amount.

A kind of 'voluntary tax' was linked with the 'Triple Assessment'. A person whose tax fell below 10 per cent of his income was invited to make up the difference by voluntary contributions. More than £2 million was raised in this way. Some of the money was, no doubt, the product of

The STRATAGEM. Alias, The FRENCH BUG-A-BO or JOHN BULL TURN'D SCRUB.

Figure 3   This cartoon refers to the first introduction of Income Tax by William Pitt the Younger in 1799. The cartoonist is critical of the innovation, and implies that Pitt is attempting to get his way by terrifying 'Farmer John' – a variant of John Bull – with the threat of revolutionary France, which is seen as a bugaboo.

Pitt supports a wolf-like monster under his arm. The monster breathes fire, and skeletons emerge with the fire. The Prime Minister declares, 'If you don't come down with your income, I'll let him loose!' 'Farmer John', terrified, tenders two bags – one labelled '10% on income', the other 'Remaining fruits of industry'. He answers Pitt, 'O, spare my life and take all I have.'

In a corner is 'A schedule of Farmer John's income and expenses', viz.,

			L		L
Pr. annum	200			Rent	40
	176			Servants' wages	60
				Carts and horses	30
		24		Tythes	10
				Land Tax	4
To support John,				Commutation &c	6
his wife and				Duty on horses, carts &c	6
7 children				Tax on income	20
					176

Figure 4 'The death of the property tax!!! or 37 mortal wounds for Ministers and the Inquisitorial Commissioners!!' The cartoon also has a label above the drawing: 'This monster was bred in a Pitt [*sc.*, William Pitt], suckled by a Fox [*sc.* Charles Fox], cherish'd in a ruined Castle [*sc.*, Castlereagh] and swept out by a Broom!! [*sc.* Henry Brougham]'

This cartoon refers to the defeat of Chancellor of the Exchequer Nicholas Vansittart, on his 1816 proposal to continue income tax for a further year. Henry Brougham, the future Lord Chancellor, and the banker Alexander Baring, led a nation-wide campaign of protest, and produced numerous petitions of complaint. The 'inquisitorial' character of income tax was a particular ground of complaint. After an intense parliamentary debate, the Government was defeated by 238 votes to 201.

Brougham, John Bull and British lion attack multi-headed monster representing income tax. Brougham wields 'Glorious majority of 37 ...', John Bull displays 'Petition of every town in the United Kingdom against the Property Tax'. Brougham says to the monster, 'Down to h-ll and say I sent thee.'

In the distance, Prime Minister Lord Liverpool, the Prince Regent (the future George IV), Viscount Castlereagh and Nicholas Vansittart escape from the scene.

honest altruism; but much was probably elicited in anticipation of favours of one kind or another.

The second important innovation introduced in 1798 might be called 'selling the "Land Tax" '. By this time, other taxes had grown so much that the traditional £2 million yield of the 'Land Tax' was less than 10 per cent of the total. The 'Land Tax' was made perpetual at the 4 shilling rate; but a taxpayer was authorised to redeem his liability and set it aside. Effectively, the Government was bargaining for ready money against the prospect of long-term yield. In the first couple of years, around a quarter of the 'Land Tax' was redeemed in this way, but thereafter, the rate of redemption was much slower and vestiges of the 'Land Tax' persisted to the middle of the twentieth century.

It soon became clear that all these devices would still fall far short of requirements and so Pitt turned to a more radical proposal, which was to replace the 'Triple Assessment'. He calculated that the total sum received in rental and profits throughout the country, minus certain deductions, was £102 million. Up to 10 per cent of that amount, Pitt conjectured, might be recoverable through a new kind of tax, an 'Income Tax'.

The new Income Tax proposals were put forward towards the end of 1798 and became law in the following year. Under Pitt's scheme, incomes over £200 a year paid 10 per cent tax, incomes under £60 were not taxed at all and intermediate incomes were taxed on a sliding scale. The annual yield was estimated at £7.5 million. In the first year, that estimate proved £1.5 million too high; but the Income Tax was retained nevertheless.

As will be seen later, Income Tax had a chequered career for more than 40 years, but eventually settled down as a permanent feature of the taxation system. In 1799, and for many years to come, it was particularly disliked for several reasons. It was seen to be inquisitorial; the declarations which the taxpayer was required to make were widely resented; it was generally recognised than many people were able to escape tax liability through dissimulation; and there were wide criticisms of the uniform rate at which it was assessed, whatever the level of the taxpayer's wealth and whatever the source from which he derived his income.[2]

Another significant change in the pattern of taxation soon arose for a very different reason. Before the French Wars, Ireland shared the same king, and a common defence system, with Great Britain, but the country ranked as a separate kingdom, with its own Parliament and taxation. In 1798, there was a serious, but unsuccessful, insurrection in Ireland, which was accompanied in its concluding stages by a rather perfunctory French invasion.

Pitt soon decided that a long-term solution to the 'Irish problem' was necessary and proposed full union between Great Britain and Ireland. After massive bribery of reluctant Irishman and considerable arm-twisting of reluctant Britons, Pitt got his way. It was decided that the 'United Kingdom of Great Britain and Ireland' should come into existence at the very beginning of the new century, on 1 January 1801. The Irish Parliament would be abolished. Irish MPs and representative Irish peers should henceforth sit at Westminster. After a transitional period, there would be complete free trade between the two countries.

Fiscal arrangements were significantly different from those reached between England and Scotland in 1707.[3] Henceforth, the expenses of the United Kingdom should be shared in the proportion 15 parts to Great Britain and 2 to Ireland. This arrangement did not imply identity of taxation systems, still less of taxation rates; it was up to the United Kingdom Parliament to decide on what items and in what manner the respective contributions were to be levied. The National Debts of the two countries differed very significantly – the Irish debt being both absolutely and proportionally much the smaller – and therefore the two fiscal systems were, for the time being, to be kept separate. Eventually, however, the fiscal systems would be fused.

Almost immediately after the Irish union was effected, Pitt's proposal for 'Catholic Emancipation', which was a collateral aspect of the arrangements, brought about the Prime Minister's resignation. George III chose Henry Addington as successor in both great offices. Pitt, however, was willing to remain until a transfer of power could be effected and even brought forward the 1801 budget under the shadow of impending resignation.

Addington has had a very bad 'press', both from contemporaries and from subsequent historians for his alleged ineffectuality; but this was perhaps not wholly deserved. In 1802, the 'Peace of Amiens' was concluded with France. Addington then sought to return to a more normal pattern of taxation. Income Tax was abolished, while the resulting dramatic loss of revenue was met, in part, by increased taxes on beer and an increase in the 'Assessed Taxes'. The 'Convoy Tax' could not continue under that name in peacetime, but it was replaced by a new tax on imports and exports. Incredibly, Addington expressed the sanguine opinion that it would be possible to liquidate the National Debt entirely over a period of 45 years by use of the Sinking Fund.[4]

Soon the British and French Governments were accusing each other of breaches of the Peace of Amiens. No doubt there were people in both countries who did not wish it to work, and any excuse was good enough. At all events, war was resumed in May 1803.

Two months later, Addington's Government restored the Income Tax, though at the lower rate of 5 per cent. One of the most powerful objections to Pitt's original scheme had been the requirement on the taxpayer to state incomes from all sources. Under the new arrangements, five separate schedules were set out, under which returns were required. As with Pitt's scheme, incomes under £60 a year were exempt from liability, but the new plan allowed abatements up to £150 only, instead of £200. For good measure, the 1803 Finance Act imposed increased duties on imports, particularly of wine. Other increases were introduced in the following year.

In May 1804, Pitt returned to office. His 1805 Finance Act raised the Income Tax to 6.5 per cent, and added to a wide range of other taxes as well. The closing months of that year witnessed the spectacular British naval victory at Trafalgar, and the even more spectacular French land victory at Austerlitz – the 'Battle of the Nations'. Pitt died in January 1806 and his death is often said to have been accelerated by the news of Austerlitz.

There was no obvious successor to Pitt, but a politically mixed government, sometimes called the 'Ministry of All the Talents', emerged, under the nominal premiership of Lord Grenville. The Government contrived to include such political disparates as Addington (who had by this time become Viscount Sidmouth) and Charles Fox, with Lord Henry Petty, later Marquess of Lansdowne, as Chancellor of the Exchequer. Fox, as Foreign Secretary, made earnest efforts to end the war; but by the time of his death in September 1806 it was evident that this could not be done. The 'Talents' did not survive much longer, and it would be difficult to discern much difference in fiscal policy between that Government and the various administrations which succeeded it down to the end of the war in 1815.

If peace could not be achieved, then more money was required for war. Income Tax was raised to 10 per cent – described by Petty as the 'natural limit' – and the exemption limit was lowered to £50 annual income. There was a further spate of taxes on consumption. For the remainder of that very long war, the rate of taxation crept up gradually rather than dramatically as new taxes were devised and old ones increased; but the overall effect was considerable. The Government was receiving about £50 a year from the British taxpayer at the time of Pitt's death in 1806, but about half as much again in the closing phase of the war.

By then, direct taxes were yielding £25.6 million from Great Britain,[5] and of that total Income Tax produced about £14.6 million. Taxes on houses and establishments yielded £6.5 million, succession duties £1.3 million, and the residue of the 'Land Tax' £1.2 million. No other item of direct taxation produced as much as £1 million.

Taxes on consumption in Great Britain totalled £42.3 million, with various drink taxes, at £22.3 million, forming rather more than half of the total. Food taxes totalled a little over £5 million, taxes on manufactured items £6 million, and taxes on tobacco £2 million. Ireland's contributions to the State receipts were still separate from those of Britain and totalled £6.3 million, of which excise amounted to £3.3 million and customs £2.4 million.

By 1815, annual debt charges amounted to £32 million, expenses on 'defence' to something close to £56 million. There were other smaller items as well, and so the figures of income and expenditure, however they are read, do not balance. The National Debt was still growing rapidly year by year. By the end of the war, the total stood at well over £700 million, compared with less than £250 million at the beginning.

When the French Wars ended in 1815, there was an almost universal wish to return, so far as possible, to a stable political and economic system. But the task of creating a new kind of 'normality' was difficult. It was taken as axiomatic that income and expenditure should balance – or, better still, that income could be slightly the greater of the two. Even if all other considerations could be eliminated, the much increased annual debt charge prescribed that the figure at which that balance would be reached would be vastly greater than before the Wars. Expenditure on the army and navy must certainly be reduced far below the wartime level, but there was also tacit agreement that the peacetime figure should, nevertheless, be substantially greater than it had been immediately before 1793. There was rapid demobilisation of enlisted men and this was one of several factors resulting in a serious rise in unemployment. The cost of supporting the unemployed, however, fell on local ratepayers rather than central government taxpayers.

In the immediate aftermath of war, several remarkable – not to say spectacular – changes in the taxation system were brought about. The change which attracted most attention concerned Income Tax. That tax, which – as has been seen – was unpopular from the start, became increasingly so as time went on. The 1815 Finance Bill was presented during the 'Hundred Days' between Napoleon's escape from Elba and his final defeat at Waterloo. In spite of the very uncertain state of international affairs at that moment, the Government had considerable difficulty in persuading Parliament to retain Income Tax for another year. Nobody – officially at least – considered that Income Tax could long survive the end of conflict, but many thought that it might run down over a year or two.

Early in 1816, Nicholas Vansittart, the Chancellor of the Exchequer, proposed in his annual budget that there should be an immediate reduction from 10 per cent to 5 per cent. As the tax had been producing over £14 million a year at the end of the war, this represented a considerable proportion of the national accounts. Immediately a great storm arose, as bankers and country gentlemen alike demanded complete abolition of this hated wartime measure. In the House of Commons, critics defeated the Government by a majority of 37, to the huge delight of crowds outside.

Such an event today would be followed either by resignation of the Government or an immediate General Election, but in 1816 administrations were less sensitive on such matters, and Vansittart, along with his colleagues, remained in office.

Indeed, Vansittart promptly went further in sweeping away unpopular wartime taxes. Agriculture was in deep recession. Soon after his defeat on the budget, the Chancellor proposed that the wartime Malt Tax, which was expected to yield about £2.8 million in a financial year, plus other wartime taxes which had been yielding over £1 million, should also be repealed. The agricultural interests were exultant and the proposals were eagerly carried.

To a small degree, the deficiency was countered by an increase in the tax on soap. This tax was particularly burdensome to washerwomen, and it was noted that Pitt had not attempted that measure even in the darkest days of the French Wars.

Such a burden on the poor could not go far towards meeting the yawning gap in Vansittart's finances, and other measures were required. As the *Annual Register* for the year records, since

> it would be necessary for [Vansittart] to have recourse to the money market, it was of little consequence that to the amount of the loan should be added the calculated produce of the malt duty.

In other words, the deficiency should be met by adding yet more to the National Debt.

Another significant change affected Ireland. Although contributions of Great Britain and Ireland towards the common expenditure had been fixed in the proportions 15:2 for 20 years from the establishment of the Union under the arrangements reached in 1800, the financial state of Ireland was particularly bad by 1816 and civil order difficult to maintain. It was necessary to keep an army of 25,000 men to preserve the country's fragile tranquility. The Government decided that the best answer was to complete union of finances. Equal taxes should henceforth be imposed in Ireland and Great Britain, subject only to particular exemptions or abatements which Parliament might from time to time agree. In practice, those exceptions and abatements were sometimes very considerable.

By about 1818, financial 'normality' had been reached. In the financial year ending 5 January 1819, gross income exceeded expenditure for the first time since the war began, and for several years thereafter both figures stood at a little below £60 million. At the same time the National Debt peaked at £844.3 million, but for a good many years to come the debt would continue, on the whole, to decline. Interest on the debt, however, still represented a sum considerably larger than all other items of expenditure put together.

There was much wrong with Britain in the years which followed the French Wars; but at least taxpayers could feel assured that they were not likely to be required to bear any great new burdens in the foreseeable future.

5 Mid-Century

Between the late seventeenth century and the immediate aftermath of the Napoleonic Wars, the volume of taxation sometimes showed violent fluctuations from year to year; but the general trend was upwards. the annual taxation income of the State had been around £2 million in 1688; it peaked at a figure not much short of £80 million in 1815.[1] Expenditure fluctuated even more than taxation income. In the seventeenth century it had corresponded closely with revenue, but growing Government reliance on increases of the National Debt made the correspondence much less close, and UK state expenditure figures peaked at nearly £113 million. When all allowance is made for the fact that the population had increased about fourfold and there had been a slow currency inflation,[2] the average overall tax burden must have multiplied by a factor of at least five.

In the 80 years or so which lie between the end of 'wartime finance' around 1818 and the beginning of the South African War in 1899, there was astonishing financial stability. Over this long period, the inflation which plagued earlier and later periods did not exist. A sovereign was literally worth its weight in gold. The UK population rather more than doubled, and reached nearly 45 million at the time of the 1901 census; while gross annual expenditure rose at a rate slightly less than population: around £60 million in 1821, £118 million in 1898.

The National Debt, which stood at about £840 million in 1820, was quite substantially reduced and was less than £570 million for the much larger population at the end of the century. Interest on the National Debt had represented about 54 per cent of the total burden falling on the taxpayer in 1818, but only about 11 per cent of that burden 80 years later.

A whole host of taxation anomalies had accumulated over a great many years, but the French Wars had increased their number greatly. As Sydney Buxton observed in 1888, writing about the early years of his own century,

Almost every article that could minister to the wants of man, physical, mental or moral, was taxed and re-taxed. The duties were complicated and differential to the last degree, the same article being often, with perverse ingenuity, taxed in different ways under different heads. It seemed to be of little account whether a duty was profitable or whether it was merely vexatious, whether it produced a threepenny-bit, or whether it produced a million sterling. It might be neither profitable nor protective, and yet be retained.

The raw materials of industry were heavily taxed. Imports of food were practically forbidden, and the prices of home produce were artificially maintained ... At one and the same time bounties were given to encourage a trade, and harassing excise duties which impaired its growth were imposed ... Duties were excessive, collection costly, smuggling rampant and fraud universal.[3]

In 1822–3, Lord Liverpool's Tory Government underwent a number of changes. These brought to the fore a new generation of politicians who were a good deal more interested in taxation reform than their predecessors had been. While none of the new political leaders could be called a full-blooded Free Trader, they were disposed to remove or reduce those indirect taxes which they perceived as unnecessary impediments to commerce. Perhaps the most important taxation change of the decade was the abolition of the remaining salt duties in 1825, but several other indirect taxes were substantially reduced. Not all of these changes were universally popular; thus, reductions in silk duties in 1829 led to riots in silk-processing areas of the London East End.

The Tories left office in 1830 and were succeeded by a Whig administration headed by Earl Grey – a government even more impeccably aristocratic in composition than its Tory predecessor. This seemingly innocuous change, however, was followed by an intense electoral controversy which led to the 'Great Reform Act' of 1832. What emerged was very far from a model democracy: about one in eight adult men, and no women, received the vote; but it was an important step in the direction of more representative government and ordinary people became increasingly conscious of their power to influence government behaviour. The general disposition of taxpayers for the remainder of the century was to look very cautiously at any proposed item of expenditure and to demand reductions rather than increases in the overall volume of taxation.

Indirect taxes were particularly unpopular. Even before the franchise was extended, there was a striking illustration of the willingness of parliamentarians to override the wishes of Ministers – even Ministers belonging to their own party – in cutting those taxes. In 1831, the Whig Chancellor of the Exchequer, Viscount Althorp, proposed a mixed budget, designed to increase some duties and reduce others. Parliament endorsed the reductions, but threw out the proposed additions. The sums involved were not large and the economy was sufficiently strong to ensure that no serious dislocation ensued, but the incident had symbolic importance, and it matched the problems which the Tory Vansittart had encountered 15 years earlier on the matter of Income Tax.

48

Nº XLI.——INDIRECT TAXATION.

MULTUM IN PARVO.

Figure 5   This cartoon appeared in the new periodical *Punch* a few weeks after Peel's 1842 budget proposed the reduction or abolition of many indirect taxes, and the restoration of income tax.

Punch does not state an express opinion on income tax, but has very decided views about indirect taxation. Specific indirect taxes are seen as demons robbing the honest citizen. 'Corn law' takes half his loaf of bread, 'Spirit tax' robs him of his refreshment, 'Tobacco duty' steals and smokes his tobacco, 'Sugar duty' takes away a barrel of sugar, other demons rob him of his soap, tallow, leather, coffee, cocoa and tea, while another rides away on his horse or donkey. The implication seems to be that direct taxation is much preferable.

THE PAPER CAP.

Figure 6 Gladstone's 1860 budget proposed repeal of many obsolete indirect taxes. These were accepted by the House of Commons, but the House of Lords rejected the Chancellor's recommendation that paper duty should be repealed.

The Conservative leader, the Earl of Derby, sets a dunce's cap on Gladstone's head. The word 'Repeal' had been deleted, and 'Paper Duty' remains in place.

In the following year, Gladstone repeated the proposal to repeal paper duty, but this time it was set out in a form which the Lords could only reject by precipitating a major constitutional crisis. The paper duties were duly repealed.

The 'Reform' controversy radicalised the Whigs in a number of directions, and the 1832 Act was followed by a remarkable spate of legislation. Some of this will be considered in a later chapter, but the new measures included an Act of 1833 which abolished slavery throughout the British Empire. Abolition was not immediate, and it involved payment of £20 million in compensation to the slaveowners. The sum was found by additions to the National Debt, not by new taxation; but it is an indication of nineteenth-century attitudes to such matters that the debt increase was short-lived and was eventually made up through ordinary taxation revenue.

The total volume of government expenditure remained remarkably constant over a very long period. For more that 30 years after 1822, it was never less than £50 million a year and never more than £60 million. As the population grew by about a third and the wealth of the country increased considerably, the burden on the individual taxpayer was becoming lighter rather than heavier. Yet the thrust of taxation underwent some very important changes during that period, which would have enormous significance for a very long time to come.

In the late 1830s, the Anti-Corn Law League came into existence. At first it operated mainly outside Parliament through the vehicle of public meetings and pamphlets. The immediate target, as the name suggests, was abolition of the 'Corn Laws'; the ultimate objective of many of its members was more or less complete Free Trade, with the abolition of most, or even all, restrictions on external commerce.

In the first half of the nineteenth century, food represented by far the biggest cost item in most working-class budgets, and corn products – particularly bread – were especially important. Among industrial workers in particular, living standards therefore turned largely on the current price of corn. This was a matter of concern not only to workers, but also to their employers, who realised that high corn prices meant high wage bills.

The original 'Corn Laws' were enacted very early in the nineteenth century; but the effect of those 'Corn Laws' had already more or less disappeared by the defeat of Napoleon in 1815. However, an Act of that year set in operation a new kind of 'Corn Law'. Importation of corn was forbidden when the price of corn was below 80 shillings (£4) a quarter: a figure which was rarely reached. When prices began to rise in the 1820s, the Government found itself caught between people who desired to abolish the Corn Laws altogether and a large section of the agricultural interest which sought to increase the rate of protection on corn. What eventually emerged, in 1828, was a new kind of 'Corn Law', based on what was known as a sliding scale. This was a tax, not an embargo. Import duties were fixed at a high level when prices were low, but dropped to a nominal value when they exceeded 73 shillings (£3.65).

At the beginning of the 1840s, Viscount Melbourne's Whig administration, which had held office for most of the previous decade, was showing most of the symptoms of an ageing government, including a perverse belief in its own indispensability. For five years in succession, State income had fallen short of expenditure; for four of those years the Chancellor's budget estimates had been proved seriously wrong. There was widespread distress among working people, with high unemployment, and high prices of essential foodstuffs.[4]

The large bulk of government income was represented by customs and excise duties. In 1840–1, the total income was £51.6 million, and those two great sources together stood at £38.3 million, or nearly three-quarters of the total. Any increase in taxation on corn or other necessities would be likely to produce an explosive reaction, while any increase in taxation on non-necessities would probably reduce consumption to such an extent that the government income would actually diminish. In the previous financial year, a 5 per cent increase in customs and excise duties had only produced about one-tenth of that increase in revenue.[5]

Eventually a General Election was forced, which resulted in a substantial majority for the Conservative opposition. After further efforts to stave off the inevitable, the Whigs resigned in August 1841 and Sir Robert Peel became Prime Minister of a Conservative Government. Peel did not combine the premiership with the post of Chancellor of the Exchequer – as some others did both before and afterwards – but in 1842 he personally introduced one of the most important budgets of the nineteenth century.

To appreciate the significance of Peel's 1842 budget, it is important to remember that a gradual change had been taking place in the character of British import duties over a great many years. Originally, they had been essentially devices for raising revenue; but, as time went on, domestic producers became increasingly conscious of advantages which – so they judged – would flow to their own businesses if customs duties were imposed, or retained, which would hamper foreign competitors in the British market. This 'protective' argument for customs duties was, in truth, completely inconsistent with the original purpose of raising revenue; for a duty which was effective as a protective device necessarily excluded foreign goods from the British market, and therefore ensured that no customs revenue was collected from them.

But customs duties, whether imposed for revenue or for 'protection', necessarily produced adverse effects on other kinds of production, for they raised the price of the goods on which they fell, and simultaneously raised the cost of manufacture of other goods. This would damage the manufacturer of those other goods and the domestic consumer alike, and would have a knock-on effect on other kinds of production in their turn. Nor was it usually possible to distinguish between 'raw materials' and 'finished products'. The raw material of one industry is the finished product of another.

Wealthy manufacturers and poor workmen alike were coming to appreciate the logic of this Free Trade argument and to see that the overall effect of high customs duties could only be harmful all round. Many manufacturers and vendors of 'protected' goods were ultimately losers as well, for the price paid for 'protection' of one commodity was that similar 'protection' would be afforded to others.

Peel was no theoretician, whether on Free Trade or on other matters; but he was a highly intelligent man who was coming more and more to see the force of such arguments. And, unlike many lesser men, he was quite willing to change his mind when the evidence so required. At first, Peel made no concessions to the Anti-Corn Law League as such, but in other respects he nosed very cautiously in the Free Trade direction.

Peel's 1842 budget made a very important departure from recent practice. Perceiving that changes in the pattern of indirect taxation were not likely to produce any substantial improvement in the balance between State income and expenditure, he plumped for a revival of the old Income Tax in Great Britain (though not in Ireland) for an experimental period of three years, at a rate of 7d (seven old pence) in the pound on incomes over £150, or a little below 3 per cent. The taxation level was set well above the income of most working class people, but it affected a large proportion of the middle classes.

At the same time, Peel proposed reductions in duties on more than 700 items. In one sense, this was perhaps less dramatic than it sounds, for a Committee set up in 1840 had decided that the vast majority of existing duties yielded very little revenue indeed. Yet the revived Income Tax meant that there was to be a dramatic shift from traditional indirect taxation towards direct taxation based largely on the taxpayer's means.

The reception which Peel received for his Income Tax proposals contrasts dramatically with the treatment Vansittart had encountered 26 years earlier. The Government's most effective argument was not a theoretical defence of Free Trade, but the demonstration that this was an effective way of turning the budget deficits of recent years into a surplus. The Prime Minister had little difficulty in carrying his proposals: a sign, surely, that a very important change had taken place in attitudes during the preceding quarter of a century.

It was necessary to review Income Tax in 1845, and again Peel took charge of the Government's Finance Bill. Continuance of the new tax was hardly in doubt; the regular deficits had been turned into a substantial budget surplus. This time, Peel pressed a good deal further in the Free Trade direction. A few export duties still survived down to that date, notably a duty on coal exports. These were all to be abolished. Tariff duties were still payable on 813 items; the new budget proposed that they should be removed from 430. The government's proposals were readily adopted. To a substantial extent, Peel had been assisted by a succession of good harvests. In the 1840s, as in all ages, the 'feel good factor' was helpful to a government.

Perhaps the most striking political feature of the early 1840s was the rising strength of the Anti-Corn Law League.[6] It proceeded to raise funds on an unprecedented scale, with manufacturers contributing a large proportion. Its propaganda had a moral, even a religious, dimension. The vigour of the League must be explained in no small measure by the genius of that great 'international man' Richard Cobden, not only as an inspired and visionary leader, but as an organiser. Cobden was an astonishing political phenomenon. He was a self-made man, with no advantages of birth or wealth. He sat loose of parties and refused office when it was available to him; yet he was universally seen in the 1840s, and for a long time to come, as a major political force.

The League had to await some event which would swing the waverers and bring final victory. That event took place in the second half of 1845 and the early part of 1846, and its cause was natural rather than human. The latter part of 1845 was wet. The English corn harvest was poor, though hardly catastrophic. Yet in the 1840s anything which reduced the quantity or increased the price of corn had an immediate and dire effect on the lives of British working people. In Ireland, the potato crop, on which the population mainly depended, was ruined by blight. Much worse was to come in Ireland in the two or three years which followed; but in 1845 nobody could have foreseen the full measure of the disaster.

Before the year 1845 was out, Peel had decided that the Corn Laws would have to go. As in 1842 and 1845, Peel himself took charge of the budget of 1846. The most famous and important proposal was for removal of the Corn Laws in stages, so that by 1849 nothing would remain but a nominal duty of one shilling a quarter (roughly 0.4p per kilogram) on imported corn. The importance of this proposal far outshadowed all others; but there were other important items, including substantial reductions in duties on many foodstuffs and on fabrics.

The passage of the Government's Bill through Parliament was extraordinary, for on critical divisions most, though not quite all, of the Whig opposition supported the Prime Minister and two-thirds of his own Conservative Party voted against him. The Bill then went to the Lords, where it appears to have been saved by the personal authority of the Duke of Wellington.

On the very night when the Government's proposals passed their last hurdle in the Lords, Peel was defeated on a completely different matter in the Commons by a combination of Whigs avid for office and protectionist Conservatives avid for revenge. Peel resigned shortly afterwards, never to return to office, and the Whig leader, Lord John Russell, succeeded to the premiership.

After the repeal of the Corn Laws and the simultaneous defeat of Peel's Government, British politics entered an exceptionally confused condition from which it did not really emerge for 20 years to come. It has been called 'the golden age of the private MP'. This state of affairs is important for the present story, for politicians were unusually open to consider ideas about taxation and other matters on their merit, and the traditional pull of party was considerably reduced.

The Conservative Party, which Peel had played a major part in establishing on the ruins of the old Tory Party, was split beyond hope of repair by the bitter personal animosities which were generated by the long debate over repeal of the Corn Laws. Peel died four years later; but the division between the Peelites and the main body of Conservatives continued long after his death. Nor was the new administration in any sense a monolithic group. The Whig aristocracy, whose leading figure was now Lord John Russell, had little in common, either socially or in their general outlook, with radicals who followed Cobden.

Russell's Government soon had to face problems which resulted from the worsening Irish famine. In 1847, an £8 million loan was approved to defray possible expenses in that connection; in 1849 and 1850, nearly £500,000 was granted to meet the problems of bankrupt Irish Poor Law Unions. Another kind of event appeared at one moment to threaten substantial taxation increases. A war scare in 1848 had stirred the Government to propose a substantial increase in Income Tax; but this was soon abandoned as a result of parliamentary pressure.

In most respects, the taxation policy of the new government was not wildly different from that of its predecessor. In 1850, taxes on bricks were repealed and there was a substantial reduction in Stamp Duties. In 1851, the Window Tax was at last repealed.

The general move towards Free Trade also continued in another direction, The Navigation Acts, which had played a substantial part in the story of Britain's deteriorating relations with the American colonies in the eighteenth century, were suspended in 1847 in consequence of the Irish famine. There was some alarm among British shipowners, but there was also strong foreign pressure to turn the suspension into permanent abolition. A consideration which may have clinched the issue was deep concern in Canada. The argument was advanced that the Navigation Acts compelled Canadians to export corn in British ships at high rates, which disabled them in competition with American exporters. Sir James Graham, one of the most influential 'Peelites', contended that repeal was essential to retain Canada within the Empire. For whatever reason, Parliament accepted the view of the Free Traders and in June 1849 the Navigation Acts were repealed.

Russell's Government had relied to a considerable extent on the toleration of Peel; but Peel died in 1850. In the following year, the new Conservative leader, the 14th Earl of Derby, became Prime Minister. The accession of Derby provided a very important test for Britain's future taxation policy. Derby and his Chancellor of the Exchequer, Benjamin Disraeli, had been two of Peel's most powerful Conservative critics at the time of Corn Law repeal in 1846, and most other members of the ministry had held similar views. A General Election held in the summer of 1852 confirmed the government in office.

The real question was whether Derby's ministry would make a serious effort to return to protection and reverse the Free Trade developments of the past decade. A *Punch* cartoon of the time shows Derby and Disraeli as a two-headed giant assailing the Free Trade citadel. Defending the citadel is not, as one might have thought, Russell or some other major politician, but Richard Cobden.

As it happened, the Free Traders had already more or less won the battle. The ministry accepted a resolution in favour of the policy of free trade, and it was carried by a majority of almost nine to one. If a government of that composition was prepared to accept free trade, then nobody else was likely to raise the cry for protection in the foreseeable future. Even the landowning interest, which had feared dire consequences from repeal of the Corn Laws, was witnessing a period of considerable prosperity.

The conversion of leading members on the matter of Free Trade did not save the ministry. Disraeli's budget, submitted at the end of the year, proposed further advances in the Free Trade direction; but there were objections on other grounds. The Government was defeated and Derby resigned. After a period of uncertainty, the 'Peelite' Earl of Aberdeen became Prime Minister. Fiscal policy was set in the firm hands of William Ewart Gladstone, who was approaching the height of his powers. Gladstone still ranked as a 'Peelite', but he was moving rapidly in the direction of Liberalism.

Gladstone's first budget, which was brought forward in the spring of 1853, proved an impressive achievement. Some important changes were made in indirect taxation. The soap duties, which bore particularly heavily on working-class people, were abolished, along with duties on more than 100 other items. As far as possible, articles of manufacture, except for finished products, were struck off the list of dutiable items. Many other duties, particularly on foodstuffs, were much reduced. The Chancellor related these fiscal changes to fundamental economic and even moral principles. The old device of using the National Debt as a device to deal with current needs was roundly condemned; far better, in Gladstone's judgement, to retain Income Tax for a few more years, despite the various objections to it. An important innovation was the extension of legacy duty to real as well as personal property. This measure produced few immediate results; but it had a significant long-term effect in reducing the power and influence of the landowning classes.

Gladstone's 1853 budget is also important in another respect, for it reduced further the differences in taxation between Great Britain and Ireland. Hitherto, Income Tax had not been applied to Ireland, and duties on spirits were far lower than in Britain. These differences were removed. In other respects, however, Irish taxpayers and ratepayers benefited from the 1853 budget. The huge debts incurred by Irish Poor Law Unions during the famine period were extinguished, and the burden of Stamp Duties on Irish newspapers and advertisements relaxed.

A lengthy and complex international crisis began in the summer of 1853, and eventually led to Britain's involvement in the so-called 'Crimean War' in March of the following year. This conflict was much the closest thing to a general European war in the period between the final defeat of Napoleon and the outbreak of the 'Great War' in 1914.

The Crimean War and its aftermath threw the taxation system into considerable confusion and held back substantially the movement towards trade liberalisation. The direct cost of the war was estimated at about £70 million, of which about £38 million was met in extra taxation and £32 million added to the National Debt.[7] Thus even Gladstone succumbed to some degree to the temptation to pass on the cost of war to future taxpayers. It took about a decade after the war before the debt was reduced to pre-war levels.

The 1850s witnessed a series of weak, short-lived governments, but at the end of the decade, stability returned. Viscount Palmerston formed a much more durable administration, with Gladstone again Chancellor of the Exchequer. Soon the march towards Free Trade was resumed. Richard Cobden, though without ministerial office, was nevertheless charged by the Government with the task of negotiating a commercial treaty with France, which was completed early in 1860. The treaty required both countries to relax their trade restrictions against each other, without imposing any obligation to impose or maintain barriers against third countries.

About the time of Cobden's treaty, an item in the National Debt which had imposed an annual charge of over £2 million on the Exchequer ceased to apply. Gladstone took this double opportunity to introduce the 1860 budget which virtually completed the Free Trade revolution, bringing the number of items subject to customs duties down to 48.

Gladstone was able to proclaim:

> There will be on the British tariff ... nothing whatever in the nature of protective or differential duties, unless you apply that name to the small charges which will be levied upon timber and corn which amount in general, perhaps, to about 3%. With that limited exception you will have a final disappearance of all protective and differential duties ...

The new commercial treaty necessitated substantial reductions in the duties which remained, particularly those imposed on foodstuffs. A small increase in Income Tax was the only significant new charge.

Most of Gladstone's taxation proposals were accepted by Parliament with little difficulty. Only one serious problem was encountered. The Chancellor had proposed to abolish the excise duties on paper. This proposal met opposition from publishers of expensive periodicals, who feared competition. The proposal nevertheless passed the Commons; but it was thrown out by the House of Lords – a reminder of the considerable power which the Lords still retained, even in fiscal matters.

In the following year, Gladstone – always 'terrible on the rebound' – achieved his purpose. Again he proposed abolition of the paper duties, but this time he was also able to propose a small reduction in the Income Tax.

All financial proposals for the year were put in one bill. The Lords could still, in theory, throw out the bill, but they could not amend it. Discretion became the better part of valour, and they reluctantly accepted the Chancellor's proposals.

Gladstone's budgets of 1860 and 1861 set the seal on Free Trade. For many years to come, nobody who counted in politics was disposed to raise the idea of Protection in any form. They were followed by massive political changes. After the second great increase in the franchise, in 1867, there were many urban constituencies in which working men formed the large majority of the electorate. By the following year, there could be no doubt that the Liberal and Conservative Parties, in the modern sense of the terms, had definitely come into existence. The two titanic figures, Disraeli and Gladstone, each experienced his first term as Prime Minister in 1868.

They were already setting a personal mark upon their parties, which has not wholly vanished to this day.

The 1860s and 1870s were decades of peace for Britain, and successive Chancellors of the Exchequer had the opportunity of introducing fiscal reforms in several different directions. They might, for example, elect to maintain taxation at what contemporaries regarded as rather high levels, in order to reduce the National Debt as swiftly as possible. They might seek to reduce indirect taxation, aiming in particular at a 'free breakfast table' – the total removal of taxes on items of general consumption like sugar and tea. Or they might seek to abolish particular taxes, among which Income Tax was most widely seen as objectionable.

In fact, all of these changes were set in motion, though to varying degrees. It would be difficult to discern much consistent difference of pattern between governments of different political parties. The National Debt[8] stood at £806 million in 1861; by 1881 it was £731 million. In 1875, Chancellor of the Exchequer Stafford Northcote re-established a Sinking Fund designed eventually to pay off a large part of the debt. The overall debt reduction was not very great in the short run, but it must be remembered that the UK population increased over the period from about 29 million to about 35 million, and therefore the burden per head was reduced from about £27.8 to about £20.9 over the 20-year period.

There were also moves towards further reduction in indirect taxation. In various budgets of the 1860s, the tax on tea was reduced by nearly two-thirds, while the tax on sugar was repealed altogether in 1874. For a time, Chancellors believed that abolition of Income Tax was a realistic possibility, and in the 1874 General Election this was an important plank in Gladstone's platform. As it happened, the Liberals were defeated; but it is interesting to speculate what might have happened if they had been victorious. In 1861, the rate was 7d in the pound (2.9 per cent) on incomes between £100 and £150, and 10d (4.2 per cent) above that figure. In 1875 and 1876, it stood at the lowest figure of 2d in the pound (0.8 per cent) for all incomes. Thereafter, Income Tax crept up again, reaching 5d in the pound (2.1 per cent) on all incomes in 1879 and 1880.

The overall taxation burden did not change greatly during the 1860s and 1870s. In 1861, the total government receipts were £69.7 million, or £2.41 per head of the population; in 1881 they were £81.9 million, or £2.35 per head. There was, however, a very definite trend, which extended over a much longer period, for indirect taxes to play a diminishing part in the total State revenue. Customs and Excise[9] receipts amounted together in 1841 to 74.2 per cent of the total volume of taxation, in 1851 to 65.3 per cent, in 1861 to 61.4 per cent. By 1881 they were down to 54.3 per cent.

6 Tithes and Local Taxation

For centuries, a substantial, but variable, proportion of the taxation burden falling on the citizen has been paid not to the organs of central government, but either to local government or to the Church.

Particular functions were sometimes discharged by one kind of body, sometimes by another. Thus, in mediaeval times the cost of relief of poverty was met by the Church, and from Tudor times by the organs of local government, while today it is borne mainly by central government. In recent times, duties and expenses relating to public health have fallen partly on local and partly on central government. Primary and secondary education has involved, and in a sense still does involve, not only central and local government but the Church as well. Many of the functions which are today administered by local government are supported by large subventions derived from central taxation.

Tithes – or teinds, as they were generally known in Scotland – are an early example of taxes which were enforced by law, and yet were not paid to the organs of central government. They were collected throughout much of Western Christendom, at least since the early ninth century. Their original function had included relief of the poor, as well as maintenance of the clergy and church fabrics. By the seventeenth century, the main function of tithes in England was support of the parish incumbent.

In early times, tithes were collected not in money but in kind.[1] A parish incumbent was entitled to claim a tenth part of gross agricultural produce: crops, beasts, even such items as milk.

During the seventeenth and eighteenth centuries, tithes developed in different ways in different parts of the British Isles. In England and Wales, and also in Ireland, there was a widespread, but piecemeal, practice of commuting tithes for money payment by agreement between tither and tithepayer. In Scotland, a settlement was achieved in the reign of Charles I, which was to endure, with only minor changes, right down to the twentieth century. Where a tenant's obligations for teinds and rent had been fixed separately, the existing proportion would remain; where they had been combined with rent, the teind would be reckoned as one-fifth of the rent.[2] Some sort of money equivalent was calculated where teinds had been collected in kind, or where rent was partly represented by labour.

In the remainder of the British Isles, tithes were a constant source of trouble for many years to come. The system was riddled with anomalies.[3] Not all land was tithable. Forest lands, former monastic lands, land deemed naturally barren and former wasteland did not attract tithes. In theory, profits from trade were titheable as well as land. Usually they were not tithed, but occasionally they were, and an astonishing case arose in the nineteenth century where an attempt was made to tithe the wages of a labourer. Tithes were not immune from taxation themselves. After the Reformation, laymen as well as ecclesiastics could enjoy the right of tithe.

As the industrial cities grew, further problems arose. They were for the most part free of tithes, which meant – among other things – that there was often no way in which parish churches could derive enough revenue to minister to the spiritual needs of the urban population. It has been argued that in England and Wales this failure was an important factor in the rise of religious nonconformism.

In the rural areas, too, new anomalies arose. Agricultural improvement and enclosure both developed rapidly at the turn of the eighteenth and nineteenth centuries, and each affected very substantially the agricultural yield of a district. Economists who followed Adam Smith were also critical of existing arrangements, arguing that the tithe burden fell much more heavily on poor land than on good.

Appearance of a growing number of anomalies in the tithing system in the early nineteenth century coincided with other kinds of challenge to the position of the Established Church. In Ireland, tithes were paid to the established Protestant Church, to which only a minority of the population belonged. Political emancipation of Catholics in 1829 encouraged them to question more openly the moral right of the Church of Ireland to derive revenue from the majority. In England, and soon in Wales, nonconformists were becoming increasingly numerous and influential. They too resented the obligation to support a Church to which they did not belong.

In Ireland, the pattern of development underwent a sudden and dramatic change during the early 1830s.[4] Farmers – and by no means exclusively Catholic farmers – began to refuse tithes, and by 1832 fewer than half the tithes were collected. It soon became clear that the cost of bringing in tithes by government action was a good deal greater than the revenue which might be secured.

By 1833, the position was very dangerous not only from the point of view of the Government and establishment, but also from the point of view of many Catholics. Daniel O'Connell, hero of Emancipation, deplored the growing amount of violence and so did most of the priesthood. An uneasy compromise gradually emerged. The Government accepted responsibility for paying arrears of tithe; O'Connell and his associates were prepared to allow that tithes should still be collected and not abolished altogether.

An Act was passed in 1838, authorising composition for tithes and making the money payable by landlords rather than tenants. In economic terms, this probably made little difference. The peasantry was more or less rack-rented, and in that sense it can have mattered little to the tenant how that rack-rent was apportioned between landlord and tithing clergy. Under the new arrangement, however, the payment of tithes was less visible and therefore less of an irritant.

In 1869, Gladstone's first Liberal Government introduced proposals for disestablishment of the Church of Ireland. The recommended change was a matter of intense political controversy, but the eventual settlement took a form which did not create too deep and lasting a sense of grievance, and the predominantly Conservative House of Lords permitted it to become law. Thereafter the obligation to pay tithes ceased in Ireland.

The earlier controversy over Irish tithes played some part in bringing to a head the long controversy over tithes in England and Wales. There were serious agricultural disturbances in southern England in 1830–1, associated with the name of a mythical 'Captain Swing'. The aggrieved farm labourers had many grounds of complaint, but one of the issues concerned tithes. Such disturbances could easily lead to even more serious trouble.

Nobody was very happy with the existing position over tithes, and several attempts had been made, under Tory and Whig Governments alike, to legislate for tithe commutation. A major measure was eventually passed, in 1836, which authorised a tithepayer to enforce commutation for money payment. By the early 1850s, the vast majority of tithes had been commuted. As with the Irish reforms, these changes did little to alter the total burden sustained by particular individuals, but they made the tithe element in that burden less obvious and politically less dangerous.

By about 1870, a sort of uneasy truce existed on the matter of tithing in various parts of the United Kingdom. A great many people were far from happy about the existing state of affairs, but there was no immediate crisis which was likely to bring about dramatic change.

The cost of local secular administration imposed a financial burden which fell much more widely than the burden of tithes. The taxation powers of local authorities sometimes derived from statute and sometimes from customary practice recognised at Common Law. There were wide difference in systems of local taxation in different parts of the United Kingdom. All local government powers, however, could be varied or overridden at any time by Act of Parliament. In contrast with many countries, there was no 'entrenched' right vested in local authorities to run their own affairs, whether for taxation or for other purposes.

In England and Wales, there were various bodies with power to impose local taxation. The parishes were responsible for relieving the poor, for maintaining the parish church and for maintaining highways. The counties were responsible for repairing bridges, and for certain expenses in connection with the maintenance of public order. The incorporated boroughs also had powers of taxation, but these powers were not the same in all cases. In the late eighteenth and early nineteenth centuries, they received statutory authorities for the erection and maintenence of goals. Some also operated poor relief on a borough-wide rather than a parochial basis.

It is not easy to say how heavy a burden local taxation imposed on the ordinary citizen in the seventeenth and eighteenth centuries, because only piecemeal information has been preserved. An Act of 1776 required overseers to make returns of sums raised in Poor Rates. This showed that the total was rather more than £1.5 million, or about 4 shillings (20p) a head in a population of about 7.5 million.[5] The State revenue for the same year was around £10.6 million, about seven times as much. A similar Act in 1803 revealed Poor Relief expenditure in 1802–3 of £4.27 million, or nearly 9 shillings (45p) per head. State expenditure for the year was £54.8 million, nearly 13 times as much.

After the French Wars, the position changed radically. State expenditure was greatly reduced, while the enormous amount of poverty and destitution which followed the wars placed a far heavier burden on parish authorities. By 1818, the sum spent on Poor Relief was

> exceptionally, nearly £8 million ... It worked out at 13s.3d a year for every inhabitant – man, woman and child – and nearly equalled the entire peace expenditure of the national government (apart from the burden of debt) in all the civil departments, omitting the army and navy ...

In addition, there were various other local charges, such as church rates, highway rates and in some places sewerage rates; while in many towns there were police, paving, lighting and improvement rates. During the latter part of the French Wars, there was also a militia rate. Thus the burden of local expenditure represented a very substantial sum for the early nineteenth-century taxpayer.

Assessments for poor rate in a parish were fixed by churchwardens and overseers, with a right of appeal to the Justices of the Peace in Quarter Session. After a period of confusion, an Act of 1739 declared unambiguously that the Justices were empowered to fix the county rate. In some cases there were provisions for visibly poor parishes to receive assistance from neighbours.

Immense problems were posed in assessing the liability of a particular individual to local taxation. Sometimes the manner of assessment varied according to the object of the taxation. Thus, sewerage rates would be related, at least in theory, to the benefit which the ratepayer derived from drainage of particular tracts of land. As far back as 1633, however, the Chief Justice advised the rating authorities:

> If the statute in particular cases gives no special direction, it is good discretion to go according to the rate of taxation for the poor; but where the statutes themselves give direction, follow that.[7]

The statute from which the parishes derived their power and duty to impose a Poor Rate was an Act of 1601, which itself was partly a re-enactment of earlier legislation. The Act prescribed that the liability of the ratepayer was to be related to his 'ability'– in modern parlance, to his means.

But what did 'ability' mean, and how was it to be assessed? Did 'ability' mean the value of a man's property, real, personal, or both? The annual income, in money or money's worth, which he derived from that property? If he was a craftsman – or, in later times, a factory owner – did it include the value of his tools or manufacturing equipment? If so, there were serious difficulties. In a case of 1775, the celebrated Lord Mansfield noted that

> Some artificers have a considerable stock-in-trade; some have only a little; others none at all … A tailor has no stock-in-trade; a butcher has none; a shoemaker has a great deal. Shall the tailor, whose profit is considerably greater than that of the shoemaker, be untaxed, and the shoemaker taxed?[8]

These problems are similar to those which have already been noted in connection with national taxation. But there was a further difficulty which did not apply with national taxation. Often, a man had property in two or more parishes. An early case established that a ratepayer could not be assessed by parish authorities in respect of property occupied elsewhere and that a landlord could not be assessed for his rent. Any other practice would have involved 'double taxation' – that is tax would be collected twice on the same item.

Thus most parishes soon came to collect Poor Rates exclusively on the value of real property; but there were exceptions even at a late date. In the maritime parish of Poole, ships' masters and clerks were assessed in respect of salaries in 1792; while in the urban parish of St Mary Whitechapel, the test in 1823 was not simply the annual rental value of a piece of property. In one case, a house rented at £40 was rated at nearly twice as much as two cooperages rented at the same sum.[9] In such cases, 'ability' was still, apparently, being interpreted to mean the whole wealth of the ratepayer. Closer inspection reveals many other local variations in assessment principles. The only way in which an assessment could be challenged was through litigation, whose outcome was uncertain; so most ratepayers probably accepted the local practice without too much argument.

Thus the principles on which an individual ratepayer was assessed varied substantially in different parishes. There were also inequalities in the county rate burden falling on different parishes, proportions often following archaic rules whose ultimate origin may well have been arbitrary. The difference between the poor rate burden in different parishes was even more marked. A parish was responsible for paupers who had acquired 'settlement' there. In the early industrial period, this led to glaring injustices. In times of prosperity and labour shortage, a manufacturing parish would gladly accept temporary incomers; but it would be equally eager to return them to their parishes of 'settlement' in harder times, when they appeared likely to seek poor relief.[10]

An Act of 1815 made what looked like a hopeful beginning of reforming some of the anomalies and absurdities. A universal system of valuation of rateable property was proposed. This was designed to ensure that the county rate would henceforth fall evenly on different parishes within a county, and also that a uniform system of valuation should be applied within each parish.

Unfortunately, the 1815 Act did not produce all the benefits intended. A county was not compelled to adopt the new valuation system, and those counties which did revalue did not all follow the same principles in doing so. Those which revalued included the main manufacturing counties – places where the rural gentry who took decisions on such matters had an obvious grievance against the apparent undervaluing of factories and habitations associated with rising industries. By 1832, 16 counties had not changed their valuation at all. Where change did take place, assessment within a parish was made by the usual parish officials – churchwardens, overseers of the poor, assessors and collectors – who had an obvious incentive to undervalue.

An even more widespread problem concerned the total Poor Rate which a place was required to sustain. There were enormous variations from parish to parish. One author has claimed that in 1834 there were

> nearly 15,000 different Poor Law authorities, and therefore that number of interpretations of the law and ways of giving or refusing relief.[12]

This is an exaggeration, for it is difficult to believe that the practice of every parish differed in some way from that of all others; but there were certainly many available interpretations of the Poor Law.

The parishes were also becoming less autonomous in these matters, and rates were becoming more uniform within a county.[13] In most places, the Justices had the right to appoint the parish overseer; everywhere they had the right to inspect parish accounts, and to hear appeals from either rate-payers or paupers. In the late eighteenth and early nineteenth centuries, they received increased power over administration of the Poor Law.

But local authorities – whether the Justices or the parish – retained enormous discretionary powers over the administrations of poor relief, and it was often a matter of massive importance to paupers and ratepayers alike how those local authorities chose to exercise that discretion.

The extent to which this power had passed from parish authorities to County Justices was brought out sharply by the famous 'Speenhamland system', which began in 1795. The Berkshire Justices decided to make grants from poor relief in supplement of wages. Legislation of the following year removed any doubt about the legality of this decision. Soon, many other counties emulated the example.

It would be naïve to suggest that the people who took such decisions were prompted simply by personal altruism, or even by 'do-goodism' at the expense of other ratepayers. The effect of the 'Speenhamland system' was that an employer no longer had any incentive to pay a living wage to attract or retain workers at the more menial grades of employment, for the deficiency would be made up from the rates. People who decided on what system the Poor Rate should be collected were mostly employers of labour as well as ratepayers, and could expect that their own wage bills would be held down to a greater extent than their rate bills would rise. The date when the 'Speenhamland' arrangements began is also significant, for the 1790s were a period when there was much reason to fear that events in revolutionary France would be repeated in England unless action was taken to remedy immediate distress.

The indirect consequences of 'Speenhamland' were more or less predictable. Local rates rose enormously. There were soon many complaints that recipients of 'outdoor relief' – that is, relief which did not require residence in a workhouse – lacked all incentive to better themselves. As the 'Speenhamland' doles increased, wages fell. Labourers who were anxious to remain independent providers for their families were forced into pauperism, which cut deeply into their pride. In some places, the incentive to work was so slight that the parish began to go out of cultivation.

Meanwhile, new paupers were being generated on a huge scale through the enclosures. Between 1760 and 1844, over 4 million acres were enclosed by statute: an area larger than the whole of Yorkshire. Many people lost their agricultural holdings; while workers who held no land at all discovered that the demand for their labour diminished drastically.

The spirit of 'reform,' which had produced the electoral changes of 1832, and then the abolition of slavery and important factory legislation in 1833, was brought to bear on the system of poor relief. The report of a Royal Commission was published early in 1834 and was the foundation of legislation passed later in the year.

The Poor Law Amendment Act of 1834 established a nationwide system of poor relief and provided the very important 'workhouse test' for recipients. The principle, in theory at least, was that those who were unable to work for reasons of age or health were still entitled to outdoor relief, but that the able-bodied could receive relief only if they consented to enter a workhouse. Conditions within workhouses were consciously designed to be less pleasant than those outside.

There might have been a measure of justice and wisdom in the 'workhouse test' if work was available outside a workhouse; but often it was not. Thus at all times, but most particularly in times of economic depression and unemployment, the whole apparatus set up by the 1834 Act came to be hated by a large section of the population, and fear of the shame and misery of workhouse life remained vivid in the minds of working-class people far into the twentieth century.

The immediate effect on local taxation, however, was undeniable. Poor relief dropped dramatically and parish rates dropped with it – despite the financial burden of building many new workhouses. Poor Rate receipts in 1833–4 were £8.3 million; whereafter they declined year by year to a figure of only £5.2 million in 1837–8.

The pattern of poor relief operating in other parts of the British Isles was in some ways very different from that in England and Wales. These differences exerted a significant effect not only on the quantity of local taxation but also on the way in which it was assessed.

English sixteenth- and seventeenth-century Poor Law legislation had parallels in Scotland, but the practical effect of that legislation was strikingly different.[14] Furthermore, Scottish local government showed much wider local variations than prevailed in England and Wales.

Sixteenth-century legislation seemed to impose a duty on Scottish parishes to maintain their poor, and a statute of 1672 established the rule that a levy for support of the poor would fall half on 'heritors' – roughly the same as English freeholders – and half on tenants. A Scottish Privy Council proclamation 20 years later required heritors, ministers and elders of each parish to decide how much money was required in poor relief beyond that which had been given voluntarily, and to impose the necessary levy accordingly.

Penalties were imposed on parishes which failed to comply. In the Burghs, responsibility for levying the Poor Rate was exercised by magistrates; but no two Burghs followed identical practices.[15]

In practice, poor relief was not generally granted by parishes, and the poor usually had to rely on private charity. Perhaps in some places this was adequate; no doubt in many it was not. For many years, scarcely any Scottish parishes established a Poor Rate, and even in 1837 fewer than a third of them had done so.[16] Not surprisingly, the countryside was sometimes terrorised by bands of desperately poor people.

Although Scottish provisions for the welfare of the poor were less adequate than those in England, Scotland was far more advanced in its concern for education.[17] In the first half of the seventeenth century, statutes were enacted which imposed, at least in principle, the obligation on a parish to provide a school, and required the heritors of the parish to establish a schoolhouse and pay the salary of a schoolmaster. An Act of 1696 extended this principle to all parishes, but prescribed that the cost should be shared between heritors and tenants.

The division of financial responsibility between heritors and tenants was the same as with Scottish poor relief; but provision of schools was universal and poor relief was not. So one might say that while local taxation in England came to follow a pattern originally prescribed by the needs of poor relief, local taxation in Scotland came to follow a pattern originally prescribed by the needs of education.

As in England, considerable taxing powers were vested in the Scottish counties. Valuations were made by Commissioners of Supply, men who were individually named by Parliament. Their functions were originally concerned largely with levying cess, or taxation, for something like the English 'Land Tax'. As time went on, they received further duties of a more local character, and remained at the centre of county administration until local government was radically revised in the 1880s.

The problem of Scottish poverty remained, and in the nineteenth century came to exert a much greater influence on local taxation. The Highland clearances, which reached their peak in the first two decades of the century, produced great numbers of landless paupers. The Union of Britain with Ireland in 1801 was followed by massive immigration of destitute Irish people, many of whom went to Scotland. Bad as conditions were for the poor in Scotland, they were even worse in Ireland, and economic and social problems posed by these Irish immigrants excited great concern.

Then, in the 1830s and 1840s, people began to recognise the link between poverty and the spread of infectious disease which affected all classes; while distress in the manufacturing districts in 1839–42 gave the question of Scottish poor relief a growing urgency. A Royal Commission was set up in 1843, and its eventual report led to the Scottish Poor Law Amendment Act of 1845. Broadly, the system established was similar to the one set up in England 11 years earlier, but the legal rights of a Scottish pauper were substantially greater than those of his English counterpart. Poor relief became a legal right, which could be enforced through the Courts; while if the relief offered was inadequate, there was a right of appeal to the Scottish Health Department. Poor relief became the main item of local expenditure and taxation, as had long been the case in England.

In Ireland, neither poor relief nor education played much part in the development of local taxation. From the enactment of Poyning's Law in 1494 until 1782, the Irish Parliament was subservient to the Parliament of England, and the brief experience of an independent Irish legislature ended when the Union came into effect in 1801. There was no obligation on local bodies in Ireland to provide either poor relief or education. In the 1830s, however, attention became focused on questions of poverty and poor relief in Ireland.[18]

As in Britain, a Royal Commission was set up to examine the problem. The Commission's proposals were markedly different from those of the British counterparts and were effectively rejected. For much of the 1830s, arguments ran to and fro, cutting largely across traditional divisions in both politics and religion.

The eventual upshot was an Act of 1838 which in some ways resembled the English legislation of five years earlier, but showed significant differences. 'Outdoor relief' was rigorously excluded, even for the most necessitous. Workhouses were to be set up; but the poverty prevailing in Ireland was so extreme that it was impossible to apply the English principle that conditions within the workhouse should be harsher than those outside. Nor could there be a principle that 'indoor relief' was available to all. Instead, relief was at the discretion of the Guardians, who were required to give preference to the aged, the infirm, the defective and children. A system of Poor Rates was established and landowners necessarily bore the main burden.

The Irish famine which began in 1845 was a horror on an almost unbelievable scale for a Western European country in modern times. Something like 1 million people, or one in eight of the population, died. Sporadic action was taken to deal with aspects of the problem on a short-term basis. The rule excluding outdoor relief had to be scrapped The Irish people who were relieved in workhouses – more than 400,000 in 1847, more than 900,000 two years later – must be counted the lucky ones. In many areas, rates were uncollectable, and local authority loans could not be repaid.

Eventually, it has been seen, the United Kingdom Parliament was compelled to come to the rescue of impoverished and bankrupt Irish local authorities.

Problems of local taxation throughout the British Isles were profoundly influenced by the development of a new kind of municipal authority from the 1830s onwards. At the beginning of the decade, the government of boroughs ranged from a fairly democratic control by ratepayers to self-perpetuating oligarchies. There were some astonishing examples.[19] In Bedford, the corporation was controlled by one in 70 of the population, who represented only one-fortieth of the property in the town. In Lincoln, three-quarters of the corporation members were not ratepayers. In Liskeard, only one fiftieth of those contributing taxes to the corporation had any control over its activities. It did not necessarily follow that a closed corporation would be inefficient and corrupt, or that a 'ratepayers' democracy' would be efficient and honest, but in general there was a strong correlation.

After the Reform Act of 1832, it was impossible to defend a system under which municipal government was riddled with more anomalies and absurdities than Parliament itself. In England and Wales, the arrangements in municipalities differed so much from each other that no satisfactory solution could be offered without a thorough survey of the existing state of affairs, which necessitated a Royal Commission.

In Scotland, instances of incompetence and corruption were at least as bad as those of England and possibly worse, yet the problem was more simple because the 'setts', or constitutions, of the Burghs were much less varied.[20] Thus it was possible to proceed with municipal reform in Scotland more rapidly than in England. Legislation of 1833 prescribed that corporations of the 66 Royal Burghs, and other Parliamentary Burghs, should be chosen by '£10 householders' – that is, by people occupying houses with annual valuation of £10 or more.

Power was given to Royal Burghs and certain others to adopt a 'police system'. This term included the function of 'watching' – roughly what is understood by police duties today – but it covered much more as well. Thus, it included 'lighting, paving, cleansing, water supply, drainage, scavenging, the prevention of infectious diseases and the removal of ruinous houses.[21]

So Scotland led the rest of the United Kingdom in adoption of a modern system of local government with taxation powers vested in elective authorities, whose activities were also made subject to independent audit.

When the Royal Commission had completed its work, Parliament addressed itself to the Boroughs of England and Wales. The Municipal Corporations Act of 1835 which resulted from these labours set a pattern of municipal government which would remain substantially unaltered for many years to come, and would eventually influence the development of rural local government as well. With the exception of the City of London and a few other places, all Boroughs would receive a similar kind of corporate structure. Councillors would be elected by all 'ratepayers' – that is, by all persons liable to pay poor rates – thus providing a considerably wider municipal franchise than with the Scottish Burghs, and a councillor would normally hold office for three years. Aldermen would be elected for six years by the councillors, and the mayor would be elected annually by the whole Council. Towns like Manchester and Birmingham, which had not previously had corporations did not immediately receive them, but were authorised to petition Parliament for incorporation.

Ireland had to wait a further five years for municipal reform. Here, the old British problems of corrupt, self-perpetuating corporations were compounded by a religious dimension, for in practice municipal authorities were bodies of Protestants in an overwhelmingly Catholic country.[22] When reform at last came, in 1840, most of the Irish municipal corporations were suppressed, leaving only ten which were to receive elective authorities. As in England, the remainder eventually received authority to petition for charters of incorporation. The Irish municipal franchise followed the Scottish rule of restriction to '£10 householders'. In practice, this meant an even narrower franchise than in Scotland, for the country was poorer.

Reform of the municipalities was followed almost immediately by a demand for comparable changes in other branches of local government. This demand would not be fulfilled for a very long time to come. A large number of powerful people who had great influence with parliamentarians of the day had a substantial interest in the existing state of affairs, and were not likely to relinquish that interest without a struggle

Yet the most important breach in the walls of the old régime in local government had already been made. In England and Wales at least, municipal authorities were already in place who had large powers to tax and to spend. The electorate for these authorities was more or less coterminous with the body of people who were liable to taxation. This precedent would gradually be extended throughout both local and national government

From the middle of the nineteenth century onwards, many further changes were made both in the system of tithing and in the system of local government taxation Both systems, however, were henceforth much more closely bound up with the system of central government taxation. New developments derived from the direct intervention of parliament, and are conveniently considered alongside other taxation changes.

7 Constructive Taxation

As the nineteenth century advanced, the United Kingdom moved further in the direction of a true democracy. The so-called 'Reform Acts' of 1867 and 1884 created the 'household franchise', which meant that nearly all adult male householders obtained the vote. The 'Ballot Act' of 1872 made voting secret. The political parties began to take on a distinctly modern aspect. Politicians came to realise that they could only retain, or secure, power by making their policies attractive to a large section of a broad electorate.

The quest for economy remained as strong as ever throughout the century, but in other respects ideas about public spending began to change rapidly. It was recognised, for example, that a great deal of illness could be averted by proper sanitation; but that this would cost a lot of money. There was growing interest in public support for education, which derived in part from a perceived need for literate people to work in industry and commerce. Traditional items of public spending, like 'defence', were becoming more expensive. All this implied more taxation, whether for central or for local government.

At the same time, the conviction grew that the organs of government both could, and should, take more positive action to relieve the worst incidents of poverty. During the intense fiscal controversy of the 1840s, many Free Traders had believed that the triumph of their cause would not merely alleviate the lot of the poor, but would strike at the very roots of poverty. But although most working-class people became more prosperous than in former times, there were many quarters where dire poverty still remained.

Towards the end of his life, Richard Cobden himself came to recognise that much more was required than Free Trade in the narrow sense of the term. 'If you can apply free trade to land and labour too,' he declared at Rochdale in 1864, 'then ... the men who do that will have done for England probably more than we have been able to do by making free trade in corn.'[1] This implied a belief that measures could be taken by organs of government which would greatly improve economic and social conditions. If so, it was difficult to see how that relief could be granted without substantial changes in taxation.

But the general prosperity of the later 1850s, the 1860s and the early 1870s made most people disinclined to support any radical economic changes, whether through taxation or other means. The general view was still that State expenditure, and therefore taxation, was only required for

BOLD ROBIN HOOD.

Sir Robin Hood H-rc-rt (*addressing "The Merchaunte"*). "NAY, FRIEND, 'TIS NO ROBBERY! I DO BUT EASE
YOU OF THIS TO RELIEVE YOUR POORER BRETHREN!"

Figure 7 Sir William Harcourt's 1894 budget was clearly designed, at least in part, to promote a redistribution of wealth. In this *Punch* cartoon, Harcourt is cast as Robin Hood, mulcting the rich 'Merchaunte' of his purse by taxation, so that the proceeds could be given to the poor.

such purposes as 'defence', maintenance of the essentials of government, preservation of law and order, public health, communications and perhaps elementary education. Those costs should be kept to a minimum, and the taxes required to defray them should be levied in a way which produced the minimum possible distortion of economic activity.

In the late 1870s, however, there were increasing indications that something was seriously amiss with the economy. Unemployment rates for the period are largely conjectural and unreliable, but they do afford some indication of how the working class was faring. Available estimates[2] suggest that unemployment figures rose year by year from about 1 per cent in 1872 and 1873 to a figure exceeding 10 per cent in 1879. The *Annual Register*, not a particularly radical publication, gives an appalling picture of the situation at the beginning of that year:

> Thousands of families, which in times of ordinary prosperity lived in decent comfort, were said to be on the brink of starvation ... The pressure was peculiarly severe on those who struggled against pauperism to the last. Many were found by benevolent visitors in a state of absolute famine, having pawned all their scanty possessions and even their clothes to obtain food.

Towards the end of 1879, there were some uncertain signs that the urban depression was beginning to lift a little; but by that time trouble of a different kind was besetting agriculture. The pebble which started the avalanche was the appallingly wet summer and autumn of 1879; a year about which British farmers were still talking in the second half of the twentieth century. Much of the English grain harvest was ruined; while in Ireland the potato blight returned and there were fears of famine on the scale of the 1840s. Happily, the worst disasters did not occur, largely because it was possible to import food from other parts of the world, most particularly from the United States.

Many long-term consequences flowed from these events. Agricultural imports, originally stimulated by bad harvests, did not drop back when harvests improved, but continued to grow. Nor did conditions among the urban population return to the old prosperity. The huge unemployment figures of 1879 were reduced for a time; but then they rose again, and by 1886 were nearly as high as they had been seven years earlier. Employers and workers alike gradually realised that the tremendous ascendancy which British industry had enjoyed in the middle of the century had gone for ever, as foreign countries began to develop factories which they filled with up-to-date machinery.

People began to cast around for new economic systems, or at least for new patterns of taxation, which might somehow allay their various anxieties and grievances. In the 1880s, a considerable number of proposed remedies attracted public attention. All those suggestions – disparate and mutually incompatible as they often were – had one feature in common. Their advocates perceived taxation changes as an important weapon – perhaps as the only weapon – for bringing about desirable change. Thus emerged the phenomenon of 'constructive taxation'.

The change, it is true, was one of degree rather than one of kind. An ancient device like poor relief through local rating might be called 'constructive taxation'. There was an element of 'constructive taxation' in the gin tax of Walpole's day, and there was a strong element of 'constructive taxation' in the general shift from indirect to direct taxation which took place from the 1840s onwards. Parliament was not only seeking revenue, it was attempting to influence the thrust of the economy and perhaps to some extent to affect the relative wealth of people in different social classes, by altering the things which were to be taxed. But from the 1880s onwards, more and more people came to recognise that the existing distribution of wealth was profoundly unsatisfactory; that the situation was capable of being rectified; and that changes in taxation should play a major part in that rectification.

The works of the American philosopher and economist Henry George played an important part in disposing people towards the idea of 'constructive taxation'. George's most famous book, *Progress and Poverty*, first appeared in 1879. The author asked why the great technological progress of recent times had failed to eradicate poverty, even in the most advanced societies. George's books were read avidly and exerted a massive influence on the thinking of the time, most particularly among radical Liberals and among supporters of various forms of 'socialism'.

George contended that the root cause of poverty in all developed societies, including those which were most technologically advanced, lay in the system of land ownership. He considered that the most important step towards rectifying the situation would be to remove taxation from the commodities and activities which were currently taxed, and to transfer the taxation burden to the site value of 'land'. George used the word 'land' in the sense in which it had been employed by the classical economists to mean more or less the same as 'natural resources'. This was, therefore, a very different proposal indeed from the eighteenth-century 'Land Tax', some vestiges of which still survived.

It has been said that George was the most widely discussed man in England after Gladstone himself in the early 1880s.[3] A growing number of people came to believe that the solutions which he proposed were highly relevant to the problems of urban and rural workers alike. As one distinguished historian has written,

'Out of Henry George by either Bellamy or Gronlund' was a true pedigree of the convictions held by nearly all the leading propagandists who set socialism on its feet in Great Britain between 1886 and 1900.[4]

Further ideas of 'constructive taxation' were soon proposed. In 1883–5, a group of advanced Liberals, headed by Joseph Chamberlain, brought out a series of articles, later incorporated in a publication known as the *Radical Programme*. This publication appears to have exerted a very substantial effect on the General Election of 1885. The *Radical Programme* was the work of many hands, and its component parts were not stitched together as a coherent policy, but it provided a general indication of the way in which radical Liberal politicians were thinking. The authors did not accept all of George's ideas, although in places they seemed to be moving in the direction of his main proposals. They certainly approved of the use of taxation for various kinds of 'constructive' purposes.

Henry George and the authors of the *Radical Programme* were by no means the only advocates of major taxation changes in the early and middle 1880s. 'Socialism' admits of many different definitions, but, however defined, it did not begin to exert any substantial influence in Britain before the 1880s. In 1883, the first substantial party with avowedly socialistic objectives, H.M. Hyndman's Democratic (later Social Democratic) Federation, issued a series of proposals for changes in taxation and State spending. Some of these proposals were similar to those which appeared later in the *Radical Programme*. In the next few years, several other socialist bodies came into existence and also proposed taxation changes as an important tool for constructing a society closer to their own wishes.

Towards the end of the 1880s, spectacular strikes and demonstrations, with strong political overtones, signalled growing public concern about the existing economic order and a determination to alter it. Some people began to talk of 'soaking the rich' through taxation. In 1889, the National Liberal Federation made proposals for a land policy, phrased in terms which were welcomed by the followers of Henry George. Two years later, the NLF's more famous 'Newcastle Programme' repeated those proposals.

Other people began to advocate taxation changes of a very different kind and for very different purposes. At intervals, even as far back as the 1860s, people concerned with industries which seemed threatened by Free Trade, began to demand special protective measures against foreign competition.[5]

By the later 1870s, there was considerable agitation for action in that direction. Complaints soon began to be raised to the effect that foreign governments were actively promoting the trade interests of their own manufactures by devices like subsidies.

In 1881, a body known as the National Fair Trade League was set up, whose object was to obtain new restrictions, including protective tariffs, on trade with foreign countries. As time went on, the 'Fair Trade' activities began to be linked with developments in other parts of the British Empire. In 1879, Canada adopted a policy of protection, which operated against British as well as foreign goods. The idea of 'Fair Trade', and the idea of imperialism, became linked in many minds, and the 'Fair Traders' began to give attention to a policy not just of protection but of 'Imperial Preference' as well. Goods from the British Empire, they contended, should be accepted more or less freely, while goods from foreign countries should be subjected to protective tariffs. Significantly, the name of the movement was changed to 1891 to the 'United Empire Fair Trade League'.

For a period in the 1880s, when the depression was particularly intense, the 'Fair Traders' seemed to be exerting real political influence. In November 1887, Sir Howard Vincent of Sheffield persuaded the Conservative conference to carry, by a large majority, a resolution calling for 'speedy reforms in the policy of the United Kingdom as regards foreign imports and the influx of indigent foreigners'.

Whatever effect these ideas had on 'grassroots' conservatives, they made little impact on the Conservative government of the day. All the old Free Trade arguments were invoked. Any policy designed to curtail imports would not only harm the domestic consumer, and domestic producers who required those imports for their own production, but it would also damage the country's export trade. The 'imperial' argument was effectively demolished in a memorandum circulated to the Cabinet in 1890.[6] It was shown that the proportion of British trade linked with the colonies had not been increasing over the past 30 years: it still stood at about a third of British exports and about a quarter of British imports. Such figures did not suggest that an active policy of 'Imperial Preference' would greatly benefit British trade with the Empire, while it would undoubtedly damage the much more important trade with foreign countries.

The 'Fair Trade' movement soon lost its original momentum. The 1890s were much quieter and generally more prosperous than the 1880s had been. Real wages were higher, and unemployment was lower, in the 1890s, particularly the late 1890s, than they had been in the 1880s. No government, Conservative or Liberal, was likely to disturb the system of Free Trade in existing circumstances.

The 'Fair Traders', however, spawned two ideas which would prove much more influential some years ahead. 'Fair Trade' was the genesis of 'Tariff Reform', which was to play a very important part in politics in the early twentieth century. At the same time, complaints about 'unfair' commercial practices initiated by foreign governments led to the idea of 'retaliation'. The British Government, the 'retaliators' suggested, might counter the 'unfair' fiscal practices of foreign governments by retaliatory fiscal measures. By so doing, it was hoped, it might be able to compel foreign governments to remove those objectionable practices and then to re-establish free trade by reciprocal agreements.

Different ideas of 'constructive taxation' began to exercise an influence upon 'mainstream' politics, under both Conservative and Liberal administrations. In 1889, George Goschen, Chancellor of the Exchequer in a predominantly Conservative Government, added an extra 1 per cent tax on succession to estates, whether real or personal, which were valued in excess of £10,000. The real significance of the measure lay in the thinking which underlay it. No doubt Goschen's main object was to draw revenue from a fairly easy source; but there was also a tacit admission that some kind of control might be exercised through taxation policy on the concentration of great wealth. The yield of Goschen's estate duties was small, but they represented a step in the direction of graduated direct taxation, and established a principle upon which others would later build.

Goschen's name is also linked with two significant measures which marked the growing interest in use of public money for educational purposes. The first arose quite by accident in 1890. The Government's original idea had been to compensate owners of redundant public houses from money which would be levied by increased taxation on alcoholic drinks – the so-called 'whisky money'. The tax was approved by Parliament, but advocates of Temperance reacted so furiously to the idea of paying money to publicans in any circumstances that the idea of using the 'whisky money' in that way was dropped. Instead, the extra revenue was deflected towards technical education and proved of considerable importance in facilitating the foundation of polytechnics later in the decade. Thus public money was being used for secondary, and even tertiary, education.

In 1891, a budget surplus of £2 million was used for educational purposes. The original scheme for compulsory elementary education had required parents to make a contribution, which could only be relaxed in cases of special poverty. The new provisions made elementary education free as well as universal. There was little opposition to the change; people of all parties had come to regard education as a national need for which the State should make provision through taxation.

The next Chancellor of the Exchequer, the Liberal Sir William Harcourt, pushed ideas of 'constructive taxation' a good deal further. Goschen had occasionally used temporary budget surpluses to facilitate permanent changes in taxation; Harcourt was able to use a temporary deficit in the same way. In 1894, there was a deficit of £4.5 million, which was due, in the main, to a large increase in naval expenditure. Like other Chancellors of the period, Harcourt scorned to use the evil old expedient of increasing the National Debt. He raised income tax from 7d to 8d in the pound (2.9 per cent to 3.3 per cent), but extended the principle of abatement on small incomes.

Far more significant for the future, however, was Harcourt's remodelling of estate duties – or death duties, as they were commonly called. It was these proposals which caused Harcourt's biographer to describe the 1894 Budget (perhaps with some exaggeration) as

> a landmark in history – perhaps the weightiest contribution to the problem of public finance of the country made during the nineteenth century. It established new principles of taxation, and it established them on so solid a basis that they have never once been departed from. Harcourt himself probably did not realize the magnitude of the work he was doing.[7]

Harcourt, indeed, had originally envisaged an even more radical budget than the one he eventually set before the House of Commons, for he had contemplated not merely the root-and-branch reform of the death duties which eventually emerged, but a graduated system of income tax as well.

Harcourt's 1894 Budget proposed to abolish the old, and largely artificial differences between duties payable on different kinds of estates – most particularly the differences between realty and personalty. This reform was long overdue. Before 1894, various Chancellors had made piecemeal adjustments to inheritance duties. No doubt many of their adjustments were, in themselves, beneficial; but the overall effect was a complete mess. No fewer than five different kinds of duties could be payable on the estate of a deceased person. Probate, Account and Legacy Duties affected personalty alone; Estate and Succession Duties affected both personalty and realty.[8] Real property was taxed on a different basis from personalty, for its assessment was related to the annual income, not to the capital value at death.

Harcourt proposed that the same principles should be applied to all estates. The distinction between realty and personalty should be removed. There was to be a graduated system of taxation, in no fewer than 11 steps, ranging from 1 per cent on estates valued at between £100 and £500, to 8 per cent on estates over £1 million. This represented not only a great simplification of procedure, but also a massive development of the principle that taxes should be graduated steeply according to the wealth of the taxpayer.

The Finance Bill in which Harcourt embodied his various proposals proceeded through the House of Commons with very small majorities on the critical Divisions, and then passed to the House of Lords. The enormous Conservative majority in the Lords did not take the occasion to throw out the Finance Bill as it had thrown out Home Rule in the previous year, and would later reject the Finance Bill of 1909.

The arguments which Lord Salisbury, the Conservative leader, advanced in favour of this course of action (or rather inaction) by the Lords were impressive, and the Lords would have been wise to have remembered those arguments 15 years later. If the House of Commons had chosen to reject a Finance Bill, Salisbury contended, this would have brought down the Government and resulted in the formation of a new one. The House of Lords, however, had no power to change the Government. To reject a Finance Bill, yet to leave the Ministry in place, would result in 'the greatest inconvenience in dealing with the public finances'. Salisbury's colleagues accepted the argument, Harcourt's Finance Bill passed the Lords without a division and the Chancellor's proposals passed into law.

Harcourt's last Budget, in 1895, and the first few budgets of his Conservative successor, Sir Michael Hicks Beach, introduced only relatively minor changes in the general taxation system. There were minor adjustments to Harcourt's death duties, but the essentials of the scheme were preserved. Tacitly, the Conservatives had therefore accepted Harcourt's 1894 measures not only as a constitutional necessity, but as a permanent financial change which they would not seek to reverse.

By the middle 1890s, an important point of taxation principle was becoming recognised with increasing sharpness by all parties.[9] Very broadly, direct taxation was likely to fall most heavily on the wealthier social classes. This applied with particular force when the direct taxation was graduated, as Harcourt's death duties had been graduated.

Indirect taxation, by contrast, was often regressive in its effect, falling as a heavier burden on the poor than on the rich. The distinction is not absolute. A tax on expensive silks or a tax on fine wines would not trouble the poor at all; but the general truth remained. Poor people must spend nearly all their income on consumption of a limited range of goods; rich people are able to invest much of their income and can pick and choose the items which they will buy. A rich person may buy more tea, and more expensive tea, than a poor person; but a tax on tea is likely to be much more burdensome on the poor consumer. As Winston Churchill put it several years later, the difference between indirect and direct taxation was often 'the difference between the taxation of wages and the taxation of wealth'.[10] The enlarged electorate of the late nineteenth century was increasingly conscious of such facts, and there was growing pressure on politicians to reduce the burden of indirect taxation and to increase the burden of direct taxation.

This view was not without its critics. Some people advocated what was called 'broadening the basis of taxation', which meant increasing the number of taxable items. The main argument for this view was that reliance on a few items of taxation presented risks to the Exchequer, and, in particular, that it could not be explained to meet special needs in an emergency, such as a war. It was widely appreciated, however, that the likely effect of 'broadening the basis of taxation' would be to put further burdens on the poor. For a variety of reasons, economic and political, no government was eager to take such a step.

In the closing years of the nineteenth century, some substantial changes were made in other aspects of taxation. The old war over tithes was revived in the 1880s, most particularly in Wales. The overwhelming majority of people in the Principality had turned to the various nonconformist denominations earlier in the century, and the Establishment Church was generally seen as an alien body, ministering to the needs of only a small, Anglicised minority.

The 'land wars' of the early 1880s in Ireland and the Herbrides produced, at first, an answering movement in Wales, but very soon the matter of tithes paid to the Established Church attracted the principal attention of the Welsh farmers.[11] The tithe question, which had been more or less quiescent for a long time, suddenly became important again, and from 1886 onwards a 'tithe war' developed in Wales.

The original epicentre was in the north, but the movement soon spread to the south. Large numbers of farmers refused to pay tithes and their property was distrained in consequence. The scenes at the sites where distress for tithes occurred, and at places where distrained property was auctioned, are easy to imagine. In parts of England, notably East Anglia, there was also some agitation against tithes, though of a much milder nature.

Eventually the Conservative Government took measure of the situation. By an Act passed in 1891, tithes became payable not by tenant-farmers but by landowners. This was particularly important in Wales, where something like 90 per cent of cultivated land was occupied by tenants rather than owner-occupiers. In practice, landlords increased rents to meet the new charge and it is doubtful whether, on balance, the tenant-farmers were significantly better off. Ironically, the Established Church, which found the new arrangements much less contentious and easier to handle than the old ones, was the principal beneficiary.

The pattern of local taxation also underwent radical changes in the late nineteenth century. Although legislation of 1835 had gone far towards establishing truly representative local government in the towns, a full half-century elapsed before comparable changes were complete elsewhere. But in 1888, County Councils were set up, and in 1894 Parish and District Councils were also established. In the next few years, considerable additions were made to the powers of these new bodies, and old organisations like the vestries and the School Boards disappeared. No single hand may be seen in these changes, which involved legislation by both Conservative and Liberal Governments, and many complex arguments over the workings of the new scheme took place. In some places there was but a single authority operative, in others there were two or three; but the citizen was henceforth faced with a single bill for all the functions of local government, through what became known as a 'general rate'.

During the period in which these great changes in local government were being made, rates collected by local authorities in the United Kingdom increased substantially. Annual receipts from their own taxation sources – overwhelmingly from rates – passed £20 million for the first time in 1876–7; they passed £30 million in 1892–3, and £40 million in 1899–1900.[12] At the same time, central government revenues were being allocated more and more to the organs of local government: £2.3 million in 1876–7, £8.9 million in 1892–3, £10.9 million in 1899–1900. By the middle 1890s, the 'average' taxpayer was paying around half as much money for the purposes of local government as he was paying for the purposes of central government.

A significant change was made which did not affect the total amount of money available to local authorities, but which affected the source from which it was drawn. Local rates were originally levied on agricultural land, as on other properties. In the 1880s and 1890s, when British agriculture was facing increased competition from foreign sources of food, a cry went up for relaxation of the burden of rates. By an Act of 1896, agricultural rates were halved and the reduction in local authorities' income was met by a grant from the funds of central government.

Ratepayers became increasingly interested in the manner in which the local authorities' revenues were raised. The ideas of Henry George were given a special twist by the proposal for 'site value rating' – that is, that local rates should be levied on the basis, not of the total value of a hereditament, but of the value of the site alone. By this means, it was argued, development would be encouraged and speculation in land values, which often held land out of use, would be killed. The idea received massive support at the end of the nineteenth century and the beginning of the twentieth. Early in 1906, a petition seeking the right to levy rates on the basis of site values and supported by no fewer than 518 municipal and rating authorities was presented to the new government.[13]

A curious local tax survived in London right down to the late 1880s. Since the time of James I, and probably long before that, the City of London had exercised a statutory right to levy a tax on coal which was brought in.[14] That tax was varied from time to time, and so was the area over which it operated; but by the late nineteenth century the tax stood at 1s 1d (5.4p) per ton, or something like 10 per cent of the retail price. By that time the area over which it operated corresponded roughly with the present-day Greater London.

Almost as soon as it was set up, the new London County Council demanded abolition of this ancient anomaly, which had somehow survived the Free Trade enthusiasm of the mid-century. With some hesitation, Parliament accepted the demand and in 1889 the coal duty was abolished.

The various changes in taxation which were actually achieved in the late nineteenth century, and the many much more radical changes which came under active discussion in that period, marked a profound change in attitudes towards taxation among people with very different political ideas. By the end of the century, it was almost axiomatic that taxation would be used in the near future to achieve results far more widespread than mere increases in revenue. Just what changes in taxation would be introduced, and by whom, was still obscure.

8 Turn of the Century

> When you put taxes, however small, upon a commodity, you make it dearer, you make the manufacture of it more difficult, the trade in it less profitable; you make it less accessible of the population and the people who consume that commodity spend less money, and add less to the wealth of the country.
>
> Sir William Harcourt, discussing the budget of Sir Michael Hicks Beach, 1900. Cited in Bernard Mallet, *British Budgets...*, London, 1900

The call for naval rearmament which had prompted Harcourt's 1894 budget was the prelude to other exceptional demands for 'defence' spending, all of which would have great influence on taxation policy in the twentieth century. In 1899, a Conservative (or, more strictly, a 'Unionist'), Government faced demands for rearmament similar to those that had vexed its Liberal predecessor five years earlier. This time, £4 million had to be found. The expedients adopted by Sir Michael Hicks Beach, Chancellor of the Exchequer, were similar to those which most Chancellors of the period, Liberal or Conservative, would have been likely to follow. He raised Stamp Duties, suspended the Sinking Fund and imposed an increased duty on wine.

A few months later, Britain blundered into the 'Boer War' in South Africa, and peace was not finally concluded until 1902. From a financial point of view, the South African War was radically different from other imperial wars of the past century. Most of those wars had been fought at a very low level of involvement of the British public in either the human or the financial sense. But the new conflict was inaugurated by a series of military disasters and was marked by the very pointed disapproval of many people at home, and nearly all European states. All this provided early warning for the British Government and public that the new war would not be so cheap.

This was indeed the case. On top of the war in South Africa, Britain would soon be involved in a conflict in China, albeit one that was much less costly. The two wars together, a new Chancellor of the Exchequer was to explain in 1903, cost £217 million, which was about twice the total sum which had passed through the Exchequer each year immediately before the war.

In his successive wartime budgets, Hicks Beach was driven to make many taxation changes. Income Tax, which had stood at 8d in the pound (3.3 per cent) before the war, was increased, first to 1 shilling (5 per cent), then to 1s 2d, then to 1s 3d (6.25 per cent). Duties on items like tobacco, tea and alcoholic drinks were raised.

The most contentious taxation proposals arose in the budgets of 1901 and 1902. In 1901, the sugar duty, which had been abandoned a few years earlier, was revived. An export duty was imposed on British coal – the first export duty for many years. British coal was such an important item in the economies of many other countries that the government felt confident that this duty would not seriously impair production: a view which was not universally held.

In Hicks Beach's 1902 budget, a 'Registration Duty' was imposed on imported corn and flour. These duties were light – 3d per hundredweight (about £0.00025 per kilogram) on corn, 5d on flour – but they touched a very sensitive spot. Did they represent the first stage of a return to the Corn Laws, whose memory was deeply hated by a large section of the British population? Hicks Beach could easily reply that this was not the case at all. When Peel repealed the old Corn Laws in 1846, a small Registration Duty was retained. That Registration Duty even survived Gladstone's celebrated budget of 1860 and was not finally repealed until 1869. Yet the dark suspicion remained that the new Registration Duty was the thin end of the wedge; and that suspicion was encouraged by the fact that people who openly challenged Free Trade supported the measure with enthusiasm.

The old expedient of augmenting the National Debt and forcing taxpayers of the future to pay for present war was followed on a large scale. After the war, it was admitted that only £67.5 million of the cost had been defrayed out of taxation, the remaining £149.5 million, or 69 per cent of the total, out of capital.[1] The annual cost of servicing the debt was increased by about £5 million.[2] Meticulous financial management had brought the aggregate gross liabilities of the State from just under £800 million in 1868 to £635 million in 1899; by 1903 all of this saving had been squandered in three years of war, and the debt was as high as it had been 35 years earlier.

When the South African war at last ended in the early summer of 1902, Prime Minister Lord Salisbury and his Chancellor of the Exchequer Hicks Beach both retired. Salisbury was replaced by his nephew A.J. Balfour, Hicks Beach was replaced by C.T. Ritchie. The problems facing the new Chancellor were considerable. As he noted in a memorandum to the Cabinet:

> Within four years, irrespectively of South Africa, the ordinary annual public expenditure has risen by 30 millions, one-third of which may be put down to army services.[3]

Thus the problem was not just to meet expenses incidental to the war, but also to deal with an all-round increase in public spending which had developed in the recent past and seemed likely to continue for the foreseeable future.

An objective observer early in 1903 might well have surmised that the question of overall public expenditure would soon become a topic of general discussion. He would probably not have guessed that Britain was on the verge of a massive national debate which was not concerned so much about either the quantity or the direction of State spending, but rather about the kind of taxation which ought to be applied in order to raise the necessary money. The matter must be seen in its context.

As has been seen, there had been a good deal of rather vague talk about 'extending the basis of taxation'.[4] This continued into the early twentieth century. It linked closely with another general question of taxation policy – the relative importance which should be given to direct and indirect taxation. The exact line between the two was not always easy to draw, but the Treasury had its own definition, and – by that definition – the relative importance of direct taxation had been gradually extending over a long period. In 1841–2, direct taxation was only 27 per cent of the total; by 1861–2 it had increased to 38 per cent; by 1895–6 to 48 per cent.[5] A more recent Treasury memorandum showed that the budget estimate for 1903–4 had pushed the proportion to 49.1 per cent.[6]

For all the theoretic interest attached to arguments for and against indirect taxation, they did not have much bearing on the actual taxes which were imposed. The shift from indirect to direct taxation has been more or less continuous over a very long period under governments of different political persuasions. There had been deep arguments about principles of taxation by people who stood at the fringe of politics, like supporters of Henry George on one side and 'Fair Traders' on the other, and there were sharp disputes about particular taxes, but there was a wide consensus among the more important politicians on the general principles of taxation.

In 1903, however, an argument of a different kind began to be advanced in favour of a large increase in indirect taxation. This time, it was presented at the very centre of government.

The South African war had given a considerable fillip to public interest in the British Empire. The man most closely associated with imperialism in the minds of the British public was the Colonial Secretary, Joseph Chamberlain. His rôle as sponsor of the 'Radical Programme' of 1883–5 has already been seen; but in 1886 he broke with Gladstone over the Irish Home Rule question, becoming one of the leading personalities in what became known as the Liberal Unionists. Like the rest of that group, he rapidly moved into alliance with the Conservatives, and in 1903 he was the most charismatic and dynamic figure in an overwhelmingly Conservative administration. For some years he had been considering ways of establishing much closer economic links between countries of the British Empire and at the same time reducing British economic links with outside countries.

This was essentially the idea to which the 'Fair Traders' had been moving in the 1890s. Many of the Empire countries were already more or less self-governing, and were free to pursue their own trading policies towards other countries. In August 1902, a Colonial[7] Conference met in London, and resolutions were passed in favour of preferential tariffs between the Colonies and Britain.

Chamberlain picked up that idea with alacrity, and a couple of months later raised in Cabinet the idea of retaining the corn duty towards foreign corn, but relaxing it in favour of Canadian corn. This would evidently be the first step towards a much more general system of colonial preference. The proposal was debated more than once and a majority of the Cabinet appears to have supported it, but there was also strong opposition, notably from the Chancellor of the Exchequer. So, for the time being, nothing was done.

Late in 1902, Chamberlain undertook a lengthy tour of South Africa, from which he did not return until March 1903. During his absence, Ritchie worked on his own financial recommendations for 1903. Whatever might be said about the long-term trends in public spending, some reduction of taxation was expected in the new budget. In April 1903, the new Chancellor proposed to reduce Income Tax to 11d, in the pound (4.6 per cent), and to remove the corn duty recently imposed by Hicks Beach.

Relaxation of Income Tax represented a loss of revenue of about £8.5 million, while the yield of the corn duties was about £2 million – a relatively small sum, even in budgets at the beginning of the twentieth century. They were but a recent innovation, and the argument for their introduction in the previous year had turned on the existence of special wartime needs, which had since disappeared.

Politically, the corn duties had been a disaster. It was widely considered that they lost the Government one by-election in 1902 and another early in 1903. In any event, Ritchie was a strong Free Trader and could never countenance the idea that corn duties should become a permanent feature of British finance, which would eventually be applied to the completely different purpose which Chamberlain had in mind.

For Ritchie perceived clearly that application of preferential duties of this kind would in truth open a huge new can of worms. Preferential taxation, he explained to the Cabinet,

> cannot be partially or fitfully applied; that is, it cannot be accorded to one Colony and refused to another ... nor can the preference be witheld from India ... the loss of revenue incurred ... must be made good by additional taxation.[8]

Thus selective remission of the corn duties, essentially designed to please Canada, would necessarily lead to a great many other preferential tariffs to please other parts of the Empire.

If Chamberlain's point had been pressed, then no doubt either he or Ritchie would have resigned. But he was out of the country and nobody else cared to push matters to the point of requiring Ministerial resignations.

Chamberlain was not the man to allow such a rebuff to pass without response. In the middle of May 1903, he delivered a very important speech in Birmingham, his political power-base. He did not publicly challenge his colleagues; but he nailed his own colours to the mast in a way which they must immediately have understood.

Chamberlain declared his concern for 'our fellow subjects beyond the seas', whom he explicitly numbered as 'ten millions'. Who was included therein? Certainly not the whole population of the overseas British Empire, which exceeded that number by a factor of 30 or more. He evidently meant the white population of the self-governing territories, notably of Canada, Australia, New Zealand and of the British colonies in South Africa. He declared his wish to retain those 10 million people under the British flag for a century ahead. Chamberlain expressed the firm view that this policy would involve concentrating on trade with the 'colonies', 'even if in doing so we lessen somewhat the trade with our foreign competitors'. This clearly implied that some kind of action was required which would not only foster imperial trade but also reduce foreign trade.

So far as the general public was concerned, matters more or less stuck at that point for several months, although there was growing recognition that very serious discussions were taking place between senior members of the Government. Then, on 18 September, it was suddenly announced that Chamberlain on one side of the dispute, and Ritchie and Lord George Hamilton on the other side, had all resigned from the Cabinet. Later, other Free Trade ministers went as well; Lord Balfour of Burleigh; Arthur Elliot; and finally the Duke of Devonshire, long famous as Marquis of Hartington. One of the Ministerial replacements was truly astonishing, for Joseph Chamberlain's son Austen was promoted from a much more junior office to that of Chancellor of the Exchequer. There had obviously been a lot of back-stage politicking and different commentators have attributed widely different motives to both Balfour and Chamberlain. This is not the place to analyse such motives; what matters here is the consequences which flowed from the changes.

Immediately before the resignations, Ritchie sent a plaintive document round the Cabinet, expressing his uncertainties about the actual fiscal proposals which Chamberlain was advancing.[9] Perhaps nobody, not even

Chamberlain, was very clear about the answers to such questions. But he had to say something. On 6 October, he delivered a speech in Glasgow which may be regarded as the initiation of what became known as the 'Tariff Reform' campaign.

Joseph Chamberlain proposed a duty of 2 shillings a quarter on foreign corn: 32 times the duty that Hicks Beach had introduced 18 months earlier, and corresponding duties on flour. Corn from British possessions, however, would enter the country duty-free, as also would maize – widely used as pig food and also eaten by the very poor. There would be a 5 per cent duty on foreign meat and dairy produce, though bacon would be exempt. In addition, there would be taxes, not exceeding 10 per cent, on foreign manufactured goods. These new taxes would be, to an extent, compensated by large reductions in duties on tea, coffee, cocoa and sugar. Chamberlain believed – though on what evidence seems far from clear – that the colonies would give Britain substantial reciprocal advantages in their markets.

Within a very short time, the whole political scene had changed beyond recognition. Balfour declared, probably sincerely, that he had no firm views on the 'Tariff Reform' question. Privately, he urged Cabinet colleagues to moderate their own utterances.[10] But there was no way of holding back eager parliamentarians on both sides of the controversy. Soon the Ministerialists – Conservatives and Liberal Unionists alike – were splitting in all directions: 'Tariff Reformers', Unionist Free Traders and people, like Balfour himself, who were prepared to support 'retaliation', but were not committed to 'Tariff Reform'. A number of MPs, of whom Winston Churchill was by far the most famous, left the Conservative ranks altogether and crossed the floor to the Liberals. The Liberal opposition, which had been more or less disintegrating during the period that followed its departure from office in 1895, was brought together in unwanted unity in defence of Free Trade, against the great apostate's call for 'Tariff Reform'.

An involved mixture of arguments and questions was raised by both sides. Would 'Tariff Reform' cement the Empire together, or would it set up tensions which would destroy the Empire? Would 'Tariff Reform' create a great new fund from which welfare measures like old age pensions might be financed, or would it impoverish the workers even further? If a tariff was effective as a protective device, did this not mean that it would necessarily fail as a device for raising revenue, and *vice versa*? If 'Tariff Reform' were applied, what would happen to British industries which used foreign imports as raw materials for their own production? To what extent was British trade really suffering from 'unfair' foreign practices, and what – if anything – might be done to counter those practices? If a tariff policy were adopted, would those tariffs be granted to the right people?

Industries which might be truly deserving to protective treatment would be as likely to obtain it as piglets competing with big swine at the same swill.

And so the debate proceeded. Meanwhile, Prime Minister Balfour was losing ground everywhere. By-election after by-election was won by his Liberal opponents. Whatever else the voters may have followed about the arguments, they perceived quite clearly that 'Tariff Reform' would mean dearer food. At a time when food costs represented a much greater proportion of working-class expenditure than they do today, the political implications were rapidly taken. Within Balfour's own party, the Free Traders became increasing suspicious of his leanings towards 'Tariff Reform', and the 'Tariff Reformers' became increasingly impatient of his refusal to declare unequivocally in favour of their cause.

The two budgets of Austen Chamberlain, in 1904 and 1905, were comparatively dull. In 1904, Income Tax was raised by one penny to 1 shilling in the pound (5 per cent), and there were also increases in tea and tobacco tax. The 1905 budget was even less dramatic. The Chancellor made no attempt to introduce the 'Tariff Reform' for which his father was busily campaigning. The 'Tariff Reformers' now accepted that it was necessary to convert the country to their doctrine before any new attempts were made to advance the cause by taxation changes.

As electoral law then stood, the Government could have avoided a General Election until the autumn of 1907; but there was no real point in so doing. Realistically, the best hope for the Unionists was that their inevitable defeat would not be too crushing, and that they would be able to settle their differences in the relative calm of opposition. Meanwhile, the Unionists might have supposed, the latent divisions among the Liberals would be revealed, as soon as they were burdened with office.

In December 1905, Balfour resigned and advised the King to call the Liberal Sir Henry Campbell-Bannerman to form a government. Campbell-Bannerman complied with the King's mandate. Almost every Liberal notable save that loose political cannon Lord Rosebery was included in the new administration. At the ensuing General Election, in January 1906, the 'fiscal question', Free Trade *versus* 'Tariff Reform', was of overriding importance. 'Retaliation' was thrust aside in the controversy. This was the first General Election for a great many years at which a question of taxation policy dominated all other political issues.

The Free Traders saw to it that there was a Free Trade candidate in every British constituency. The new Labour Representation Committee (LRC), the future Labour Party, included many eager supporters of Free Trade, and a substantial number of LRC candidates stood without Liberal opposition.

In the south of Ireland, the Nationalist Party did what it could to pretend that the 'Tariff Reform' question was more or less irrelevant to Irish interests, while the northern Unionists, who were equally anxious to avoid any risk of being fatally split on the issue, also tended to brush the matter aside as far as possible. So in Ireland the new issue of 'Tariff Reform' *versus* Free Trade was not allowed to replace the old issue of Unionism *versus* Nationalism, with its strong religious overtones.

The result in the United Kingdom as a whole was a huge majority for the Free Traders in general and the Liberals in particular. The Liberals secured far more seats than all other political groups put together, Balfour himself was unseated in East Manchester, but scrambled home later in the City of London. Only in Chamberlain's Birmingham, where every one of the nine constituencies returned a 'Tariff Reformer', did Government supporters have much immediate cause for jubilation.

Other features of the election were profoundly significant for the future. As soon as the new Parliament met, the LRC formally transformed itself into the Labour Party.[11] Within the Unionist ranks, committed 'Tariff Reformers' far outnumbered Unionist Free Traders and Balfourite 'Retaliationists' together.[12]

9 Radicalism

The Liberals who had just won such a spectacular victory were a very different party from the one that had departed miserably from office in 1895. Social issues were vastly more important in the minds of the politicians than they had been a decade earlier. Deep poverty was perceived not as an inevitable feature of society, but as an avoidable evil. Many Liberals – indeed, some people in all parties – were keen supporters of the idea of introducing old age pensions. Such policies presupposed substantial increases in taxation. There was also a growing concern among the younger Liberals to bring about a much more equitable taxation system. The idea that Income Tax should be graduated – from which idea Harcourt had shied away in 1894 – was now almost axiomatic. Many Liberals gave eager support to the much more radical principle of land value taxation.

The first budget of the new régime was introduced by the Chancellor of the Exchequer, H.H. Asquith, in April 1906. This followed so swiftly after the General Election that it was not possible to introduce great taxation changes. Asquith, however, had the benefit of a surplus of £3.5 million and was able to give some satisfaction by abolishing the coal export tax which Hicks Beach had introduced as a wartime measure in 1901, but which had somehow hung on for four years after the war ended. He was also able to reduce the tea duty from 6d to 5d (about 2p) a pound.

Asquith's 1907 budget was more radical. The economy was still prosperous and the Chancellor calculated that, with existing taxation, there would be a substantial surplus. This time, indirect taxation was not changed, but there were important changes in direct taxation. Estate duties were increased in the higher brackets, while – more important – there were substantial changes in the structure of income tax. This was still very much a 'minority' tax in the twentieth century. The number of Income Tax payers in 1905 has been estimated at about one million.[1] With incomes below £2,000 a year – a very comfortable middle-class salary in those days – the 1907 budget made a distinction between 'earned' income, which was charged at a reduced rate of 9d in the pound (3.75 per cent), and 'unearned' income, which was still taxed at the old rate of one-shilling (5 per cent).

In the early spring of 1908, Campbell-Bannerman fell ill, resigned and died shortly afterwards. In the new administration, Asquith became Prime Minister and David Lloyd George became Chancellor of the Exchequer. Asquith had already reached an advanced stage in preparation for the 1908 budget, and it was he, not the new Chancellor, who introduced that budget shortly afterwards.

Asquith's 1908 budget was less dramatic than that of the previous year. The most important taxation change was a very substantial reduction in sugar duties. What attracted far more attention was the Prime Minister's announcement of the Government's intention to introduce old age pensions. The idea was quite an old one. It had been discussed in the 1895 General Election, and there were Cabinet memoranda on the subject around the very beginning of the Boer War in 1899.[2] War requirements, however, received priority. Joseph Chamberlain had originally considered linking old age pensions with 'Tariff Reform',[3] but later dropped the idea. There remained, nevertheless, some interest among 'Tariff Reformers' in the notion that pensions might eventually be financed from tariff revenues.

The new scheme was a pilot and had the potential of great extension later. A weekly pension of 5 shillings (£0.25) a week, or 7s 6d (£.0.375) for a married couple, was granted to people at age 70 who were of good character and without other substantial financial means. It was calculated that old age pensions would cost £6 million in a full year – an underestimate, as it turned out – but they would not be introduced until the beginning of 1909, and so the cost in the financial year 1908–9 would be small. Thereafter, the sums paid, the conditions of payment and the age of receipt were varied from time to time; but the essential idea that most people over a certain age should receive payment from the State was never impugned by any important body of opinion.

Old age pensions, the first instalment of modern 'welfare' legislation, are significant for the present study not only as an addition to the taxpayer's burden, but also as a shift of that burden from local to central government. Hitherto, public support for the indigent had come mainly through local rates; now, a major contribution was made by the State from money deriving from national taxation.

When Lloyd George came to introduce his celebrated first budget in April 1909, it was necessary, for the first time, to meet the cost of old age pensions for a full financial year. In addition, a major programme of naval rearmament had commenced to counter a perceived threat from Germany. Further new kinds of spending were also envisaged, including a central government fund for road maintenance. To make the Chancellor's task even more difficult, trade conditions were poor, and so revenues from existing taxation, both direct and indirect, were likely to fall. Something like £14.2 million[4] more revenue was required in the new taxation year to meet requirements. Old age pensions were expected to cost £7 million in the coming year, the navy would cost a further £3 million and there were

94

THE ARTFUL HUNTER.

"Mr. Lloyd George, under cover of a Finance Bill, is endeavouring to secure the acceptance by Parliament of legislative proposals very similar to, if not identical with, those which were rejected by the House of Lords last year."—(Mr. Walter Long.)

Figure 8 The *Pall Mall Gazette* was one of the first newspapers to carry political cartoons. Its politics had at one time been Liberal, but it was later acquired by a Conservative group. Like its Liberal counterpart, the *Westminster Gazette*, the *Pall Mall Gazette* was aimed at a small, but influential, readership.

Lloyd George, 'the artful hunter', looks for a victim on the African plains. He disguises himself with a cut-out ostrich, 'Finance Bill', in order to approach his prey. The text, from the prominent Conservative Walter Long, suggests that the Chancellor's aim was 'to secure the acceptance by Parliament of legislative proposals very similar to, if not identical with, those which were rejected by the House of Lords last year'.

Lloyd George's judgement was probably right, and the popular contrary view that Lloyd George was seeking an issue on which the mass of voters would support the Liberal government in conflict with the Lords was wrong. The government had made two recent attempts to secure valuation of all land in Scotland, with the intention of later taxing land values. On both occasions the government's intention was frustrated by the House of Lords.

This time, Lloyd George intended to avoid the mistake of introducing a separate land valuation Bill. Instead, he hoped to slip his land valuation proposals into the budget, in the anticipation that the Lords would reluctantly accept them along with the taxation proposals, just as they had accepted other distasteful budget proposals in the past.

Matters did not work out that way. The House of Lords eventually took the dramatic step of rejecting the budget. This precipitated a major crisis, and eventually resulted in a dramatic reduction in the power of the House of Lords, especially in financial matters.

several other smaller requirements, while a substantial reduction in the yield of some existing taxes was anticipated.

This was not just a tremendous challenge to the Chancellor, it was crucial for the whole future of Free Trade finance. Soon after the 1906 election, Balfour more or less capitulated to Joseph Chamberlain on the 'Tariff Reform' issue. Later in the same year, Chamberlain had a stroke, and it was soon obvious that he could never take ministerial office again; but the Unionists were by then firmly committed to the cause of 'Tariff Reform'.

By the beginning of 1909, the whole political scene had changed dramatically. Bad trade conditions disposed ordinary electors to turn against the Government of the day, as they nearly always do. Seven Liberal seats were lost to the opposition in 1908. The Unionists had every reason to expect that if a General Election could be forced, the Government would lose much ground, and perhaps be driven from office altogether.

The personality of the Chancellor was of vital importance in what happened next. Not only was Lloyd George a radical by temperament and conviction, but as a politician he saw that the best hope for the Liberals was a radical budget which would rally the country to the government's side. It is often claimed that he had immense difficulties with some of his Cabinet colleagues in getting that budget accepted.[5] That may be so; but it is worth noting that many of the patches of evidence to that effect, from Lloyd George himself and from others, were written long after the event when a great deal of water had flowed under many bridges, carrying much flotsam of political malice with it.

Lloyd George's 1909 budget was exceptionally wide-ranging. He had an eye to the distant future as well as the current taxation year, for most of the new taxation was of a kind which could easily be stepped up in the future should circumstances so require.

In the financial year 1909–10, Lloyd George proposed that death duties should be increased to raise a further £2.85 million, while additions to the various duties on alcohol and tobacco would bring in £6.1 million more.

Substantial changes were to be made in Income Tax, which were designed to produce a further £3.5 million. In one respect there was actually a relaxation here, for the Chancellor proposed that an allowance of £10 for each child under 16 should be made on incomes under £500 a year. Asquith's 'earned income' allowance was preserved. The rate of 1 shilling in the pound (5 per cent) would be retained for lower incomes, while at higher levels the rate would be increased to 1s 2d (5.8 per cent). A new Super Tax of 6d in the pound (2.5 per cent) would be levied, in addition to Income Tax, on incomes over £5,000. Super Tax would be payable on the amount by which these high incomes exceeded £3,000.

In addition to these taxes, there would be additions to Stamp Duties. Taxes on motor vehicles and petrol were introduced for the first time. The yield of these taxes, however, was earmarked for road improvements.

These various proposals together constituted the vast bulk – more than 96 per cent – of the extra taxation proposed by Lloyd George in April 1909. They certainly provoked comment and criticism; but the public attention they attracted was far less than the attention given to one new item – land taxation. The total sum which the Chancellor proposed to levy from this source in the finanical year was around £0.5 million. Those tiny taxes, and the valuation which was linked with them, were to prove of critical importance in sparking off the greatest constitutional crisis of the twentieth century, and their significance can only be understood in a wider context.

The idea that land reform lay at the root of all fundamental social reform remained as a durable legacy of Henry George's writings and visits. Land value taxation was widely seen among Liberal and Labour activists as the most vital ingredient of that reform. In Scotland, land value taxation attracted even wider support than in England, and a very substantial majority of Scottish MPs was firmly committed to the idea. On the face of it, there was much to be said for a pilot scheme in Scotland. But any general scheme of land taxation, whether for local or for national purposes, required valuation first. In the first two years of the Liberal Government, two bills to value the land in Scotland with a view to eventual taxation had passed the Commons with large majorities. Both were then wrecked by landed interests in the House of Lords. There was every reason to think that a similar measure applicable to Britain as a whole would meet a similar fate.

Lloyd George, whose earliest recorded public activity had been in connection with the Welsh land and tithe agitation of the 1880s, was sympathetic with the land taxers. In a Cabinet memorandum, he pointed out that

> The overwhelming majority of the [Liberal] Party in the House are pledged to the taxation of land values, and urgently press it upon the government.[6]

But how could land values be assessed, and then taxed, in the teeth of implacable opposition from the House of Lords? As the law then stood, the Lords had the power to throw out any bill, financial or otherwise, which had been presented to them by the House of Commons. When the Lords wrecked the two Scottish land valuation bills they angered many people, but no one could reasonably suggest that they exceeded constitutional propriety or the customary limits of their powers. There was, however, a strong tradition that the Lords would not interfere with the annual Finance Bill. They had, for example, accepted Harcourt's budget of 1894, which most of them obviously disliked.

Lloyd George proposed to introduce certain land taxes which could be collected fairly easily in existing conditions. There would be a 20 per cent tax on unearned increment in land values, payable when the land changed hands. A Capital Tax of 1/2d in the pound (just over 0.2 per cent) would be charged on undeveloped land, and there would be a 10 per cent reversion duty on any benefit passing to a lessor at the end of a lease. Another new tax proposed by the Chancellor, which is generally considered apart from the land taxes proper, was a mineral rights duty of 1 shilling in the pound (5 per cent) on mining royalties and wayleaves, whose proceeds were to be used to finance a Miners' Welfare Fund.

Another element of Lloyd George's land proposals would eventually prove of much greater importance. There would be a general valuation of land throughout Great Britain. The Chancellor's idea was evidently to slip in this valuation in a way which the Lords would accept. His aim was to circumvent the Lords, not to pick a quarrel with them.

At first, it looked as if matters would follow that course. The budget certainly excited lively opposition – partly from Unionists, partly from Irish Nationalists who fought vigorously against the added liquor taxes. Nobody was particularly exercised by the land taxes proposed for the current financial year; but landowners were deeply concerned about the implications of land valuation, which was undoubtedly intended to lead to a general system of land value taxation in a few years' time. Some MPs on the Government side were also far from happy, and in June, on the Second Reading division, 33 Liberal and Labour MPs were absent unpaired.[7] The Finance Bill was fought more or less inch by inch through the House of Commons. A few concessions were made by the Government, notably on certain aspects of the land taxes; but nobody really doubted that the main proposals would eventually pass the Commons.

In the summer, several important developments occurred on both sides. A 'Budget Protest League' was founded on the Unionist side, which was countered soon afterwards by a 'Budget League' on the Government side, whose main inspiration was Winston Churchill. By-elections were fought in the shadow of the budget and the record was much better, from the Government's point of view, than their gloomy experiences a few months earlier.

Late in July, Lloyd George delivered a famous speech at Limehouse, in the East End of London. The Chancellor treated his landowning opponents with ridicule rather than venom; but he certainly went a good deal further in his criticisms than senior Ministers of the time were wont to do, and 'Limehousing' roused fury on the opposition side. As the season advanced, obscure peers began to make speeches which were so obviously related to their own perceived interest in the matter of the land taxes that they must have been a high embarrassment to the opposition leaders. By this time, both sides were plainly spoiling for a great showdown.

What would happen when the Finance Bill of 1909 reached the House of Lords? Early reactions of Balfour, and of Lord Lansdowne, Unionist leader in the Lords, had not suggested that they contemplated any profound departure from long-established practice of permitting the Government's financial proposals to pass into law. Wise and experienced Unionists like Lord St Aldwyn continued to advise their party in that sense.[8]

The most effective pressure for the Lords to reject the budget seems to have come from eager advocates of 'Tariff Reform' rather than smouldering landlords. Perhaps Balfour and Lansdowne were compelled to recognise that the damage which would follow within their own party if they pressed the Lords to accept the budget would be even greater than the electoral damage which would follow if they advised them to reject it. Balfour's principal biographer dates the Unionist leader's eventual decision to recommend the Lords to throw out the Budget to a date in early August,[9] and the first authoritative public statement to that effect came in the following month. In the end, the Lords threw out the Budget by 350 votes to 75.[10] No government could ignore such a challenge. Parliament was dissolved and in January 1910 polling took place. There was a clear understanding that, if the budget secured a majority in the new House of Commons, the Lords would let it through.

At the General Election which followed, taxation policy was the overriding issue. The budget was the immediate topic, but there were also echoes of the old argument over Free Trade and 'Tariff Reform'.

The result of that General Election can hardly have satisfied either the Government or the opposition. The Liberals lost ground and finished up almost exactly level with the Unionists: 275 seats against 273. The Unionists were far short of the majority which had seemed well within their grasp a few months earlier. The 40 Labour MPs could for most purposes be added to the Liberal total, while the Irish Nationalists, with an almost unchanged representation of 82, now held the balance of power. This would prove a most doubtful boon. In the old Parliament, they had sometimes voted against the budget and sometimes abstained. Now the issue before them was not so much the budget as the long-term prospect of Home Rule. If the budget was defeated, the Government would have to resign and the Unionists – whose very name proclaimed their continuing opposition to Home Rule – would take over. Most Irish Nationalists eventually decided to support the budget, in the hope that they would eventually be able to cajole the

Liberals into granting Home Rule. A significant minority chose to vote with the opposition.[11] No MP from any of the three British parties cross-voted, and the Finance Bill passed its critical Second Reading by 330 votes to 244. The Lords then let it through without a division.

While this long, convoluted process was taking place, ordinary taxation was in a state of chaos. As the law then stood, the only taxes which could lawfully be demanded were those which had been authorised in 1908. Thus there was an enormous deficit for the year 1909–10: expenditure £157.9 million, receipts £131.7 million. As soon as the Finance Bill of 1909 passed into law, in April 1910, it became possible to collect the missing £26.2 million, but, during the interim, suspension of the Sinking Fund and substantial borrowing had been necessary.

Passage of the Finance Bill was by no means the end of the turmoil. Almost immediately the political world was plunged into another crisis almost as involved and exciting as the previous one, at the end of which the House of Lords grudgingly accepted a reduced constitutional rôle, with formal acknowledgement that it had no power to impede a 'Money Bill' which had passed the Commons.

In 1911, a second major item of 'welfare' legislation was set before Parliament: the National Insurance Bill. The essential idea was that a new fund should be set up, into which contributions should be made simultaneously by workers, employers and the State. From this fund, workers or their personal representatives would be entitled to draw in event of illness, disability, maternity or death. The scheme as originally operated applied only to people earning less than £150 a year – which included the great majority of manual workers. Initially, the worker's contribution was 4d a week (1.7p) for men and 3d for women; the employer's contribution 3d (1.25p) and the State contribution 2d (0.8p). Thus Lloyd George was able to argue that the scheme represented – from the worker's point of view – 'ninepence for fourpence'.

Linked with the health provisions of the National Insurance Bill were provisions for further contributions for unemployment insurance. The scheme was compulsory in certain industries, notably building and mechanical engineering, and – as time went on – was extended to others. Contributing workers were entitled to payment for a limited period of unemployment.

The National Insurance Bill had a stormy parliamentary history. Some people objected to the whole idea; some declared that the scheme should not be contributory but should be paid for entirely out of taxation. The numerous door-to-door insurance agents operating in working-class districts had to be reassured that their jobs were not at risk; friendly societies and trade unions who operated insurance schemes of their own had to be mollified; doctors had to be reassured that professional relations with patients would not be impaired.

In the end, however, the measure passed into law more or less as originally intended. The amounts of contributions, and the benefits received, were varied from time to time in the years which followed, and it would be tedious to relate the details here. But important considerations, practical and theoretical, must concern the historian of taxation.

There was a contribution by the State, drawn from ordinary taxation. The compulsory contributions of employers might be regarded as a kind of payroll tax. But were the compulsory payments of workers really to be regarded as a sort of poll tax, or as genuine insurance premiums?

There was a further theoretical difficulty. Some people, including many self-employed men, were free to enter the National Insurance scheme if they wished, but were not compelled to do so. Was the compulsory payment made by a worker employed by somebody else a form of taxation, while the contribution made by his self-employed brother, working at a similar occupation and for a similar emolument, was something fundamentally different – a voluntary insurance premium? As the welfare state developed, lines became increasingly blurred.

As with old age pensions, National Insurance involved a shift of burden from local to national taxation. Payments to workers under the scheme necessarily implied that there would be fewer demands for payments under the Poor Law, whose burdens had fallen on the local ratepayer.

Other welfare provisions of the period were providing expenditure which derives unambiguously from true taxation, but the source of that taxation changed. Thus, in 1906, local authorities were empowered to provide free school meals for certain children. In 1914, the cost of such meals ceased to fall exclusively on local rates, but half was defrayed by central government.

However taxation is defined, the overall effect of these changes on the taxation system was massive by contemporary standards. In 1901, the main kind of welfare had been poor relief, for which around £9 million a year was collected by local authorities. Thereafter, poor relief only increased to a relatively small extent – by the outbreak of war in 1914 it was running at about £12 million. But the payments which were made by the State for such items as health and insurance, negligible or non-existent at the beginning of the century, were not much short of £20 million.

The consequences of two and a half years of intense political excitement were very different from what the eager partisans of either side had anticipated. Lloyd George's next few budgets were tame affairs, making practically no change to the measures which had been accepted in the spring of 1910. Even the National Insurance Act which Parliament passed in 1911 did not require sufficient funds to render major new taxation necessary.

In the next three years, public attention moved largely from questions of taxation to other issues, notably Irish Home Rule, possible extension of the franchise to women, and to some intense industrial disputes, with syndicalist overtones. But by-election results – the Hanley contest of August 1912 was the most spectacular – showed that land taxing had an immense popular appeal. This excitement certainly had nothing to do with the yield of those new land taxes which had actually been imposed, which was minuscule. The mineral rights duty, it is true, was moderately productive, and by the end of the 1913–14 financial year it had yielded nearly £1.6 million. Yet at that date the land value duties proper had only produced a little over £0.6 million. The valuation, by contrast, had cost over £2 million to date,[12] and was employing 5,000 staff, while a substantial part of the country had not been covered. To this matter it will be necessary to return later.

Lloyd George's last pre-war budget, in May 1914, made another attempt to introduce radical changes in both taxation and expenditure. Again, there was a demand for increased naval spending, while this time attention was focused also on problems of local authority expenditure and taxation, once the land valuation was complete. The Chancellor contemplated that the basis of the local rating system should be switched from the traditional assessment of the total value of a hereditament to assessment of the site alone. The Government proposed to supplement local spending by substantial government grants. Poor law payments, police, public health and education expenses of local authorities were all to receive very substantial subventions from central taxation sources. The new requirements would result in a further increase in the higher ranges of income tax and death duties.

The 1914 budget had a turbulent parliamentary history. The Government encountered considerable difficulty with some of its own supporters, and substantial concessions were made. It eventually received Royal Assent at the end of July. By that time, few people were very interested in the whole debate, for everybody in politics was preoccupied with the double crisis of the late summer. The Government's Irish Home Rule legislation was on the point of enactment, and many people apprehended much violence in Ulster as soon as it took effect. This grave problem was then overtaken by an even graver matter, with the sudden rush of events towards international war.

Some general conclusions might be drawn about developments in public expenditure and taxation in the period leading to the 1914 war. Government spending had been rising over a very long period: £55.8 million in

1853–4; £74.6 million in 1873–4; £98.5 million in 1893–4. In 1914–15, for the first time, spending was scheduled to exceed £200 million.

To some extent, the rise in taxation was attributable to a rising population, which had increased by about two-thirds over the 60-year period; but this was not the principal explanation. Government spending, most particularly on the navy, social welfare and education, was rising at a much greater rate than population. The navy had cost £7.8 million in 1853–4; in 1913–14 it cost £48.8 million. Army costs grew as well, but less rapidly: £9.4 million in 1853–4, £28.3 million in 1913–14. Over the same period, the general costs of civil government, which included both social welfare and education, had risen from £7.2 million to £56.8 million. The only major item on which the public burden had been substantially reduced was National Debt charges: £28 million in 1853–4, £19.3 million in 1913–14.

Receipts and spending of local government authorities followed a pattern somewhat similar to that of central government. Figures from the early period are incomplete; but in 1882–3 the total rate receipts of local authorities in the United Kingdom were £30.5 million, while in 1913–14 they stood at £82.4 million.

The change from indirect to direct taxation during the nineteenth century has already been noted. That change continued into the early twentieth century. By 1912–13, direct taxation (as defined by the Treasury) exceeded indirect taxation by the substantial margin of 57.6 per cent to 42.4 per cent.[13] Another important change was the graduation of direct taxation. This development was related to the view that taxation should be used not merely to raise revenue but to redistribute wealth. No doubt the Liberals, on the whole, welcomed that process more than the Unionists did; but no serious politician in any party was likely to reverse the change once it had taken place.

Yet on the eve of the 1914 war, the tax burden still fell in a very uneven manner.[14] The proportion of income collected in indirect taxation dropped regularly as income advanced and the proportion collected in direct taxation increased; but when the total tax burden is considered, the pattern becomes more complex. A married man with three children, whose income was only £50 a year, was likely to be paying 8 percent of that tiny wage in taxation. As income increased, this proportion dropped rapidly, reaching 4 per cent at £200 a year – the level of a very comfortable artisan or a moderately successful small shopkeeper. Thereafter it rose; but the very poor man's level of 8 per cent was not reached again until the taxpayer attained the extremely affluent level of £10,000. The reason for this curious pattern was the huge burden of taxes which the poor still paid on just four items: tea, sugar, tobacco and alcoholic drinks.

10 War and After

When Britain went to war in August 1914, nobody doubted that the conflict would be very expensive; but the cost rapidly passed all anticipation. In November 1914, the Chancellor of the Exchequer, Lloyd George, foretold that the war would cost at least £450 million in the first full year – that is, a little over £1.23 million a day. On 1 March 1915, Prime Minister Asquith predicted that the cost would be more than £1.7 million a day during the forthcoming year. At the beginning of May 1915, Lloyd George told the House of Commons that the average daily cost of the war – excluding loans to Allies and Dominions – was £2.1 million a day. This was substantially more than twice the total government expenditure at any previous time. In June, Asquith estimated that expenditure in the succeeding months would run at £3 million a day. In November, the Prime Minister considered that the 'outside estimate' of war costs had now risen to £5 million a day. So, over a period of 12 months, official estimates of the daily cost of the war had multiplied by a factor of four. In April 1918, Bonar Law, who by then had become Chancellor, estimated a daily expenditure in excess of £8 million. There is no reason for thinking that any of these men was deliberately misleading Parliament.

Just four days after Britain went to war, the first major departure from traditional financial practice was made. On 8 August 1914, Parliament granted a Vote of Credit for £100 million. A Vote of Credit authorises the administration to spend the sum granted as it sees fit, within very broad limits. It is therefore different from ordinary Estimates, or Supplementary Estimates, which are earmarked for a particular purpose. Votes of Credit had long been unpopular among strict economists in all parties, because of the great power which they gave to an administration. On this occasion, however, there was no serious objection to the proposal. Thereafter, Votes of Credit continued to be granted every few months and for rapidly increasing sums.

Later in August 1914, an even greater financial change was made. The Treasury had been given unlimited borrowing powers – the clearest possible warning that the National Debt would also no longer be kept under any sort of effective control.

The first wartime budget, which was introduced by Lloyd George in November 1914, gave a clear indication of the way in which the war would be financed. The Chancellor proposed additions to current taxation in order to meet wartime needs; but these additions were modest by comparison with the anticipated new expenditure. Income Tax and Super Tax would be doubled almost immediately, but the increased rate of taxation would apply for only the remaining part of the current financial year. The effect was to collect Income Tax over the whole financial year 1914–15 at the rate of 1s 8d in the pound (8.3 per cent) on unearned income, and 1 shilling in the pound (5 per cent) on earned income.

The tax on tea was to be raised from 5d a pound to 8d, and the tax on beer would be increased by about a penny a pint. New taxation was expected to raise, in total, about £15.5 million towards the massive sum required in the current financial year, while partial suspension of the Sinking Fund would save rather more than £2.7 million.

Even on the Chancellor's sanguine estimates, taxes on that scale would not go far towards meeting the cost of war. He calculated that there would be a deficit of almost £340 million by the end of the financial year. The Chancellor suggested that if taxation were levied at the highest rate which had been collected during the French Wars, that sum would have sufficed to meet requirements; but he evinced no intention of making similar demands on the current occasion. The enormous gap between taxation income and expenditure could only be bridged by borrowing on a massive scale. The earlier decision to give the Treasury unlimited borrowing powers would plainly be exploited to the full.

The parliamentary debate which ensued provided no indication that other parties took a greatly different view from the government. As the Finance Bill passed swiftly through the House of Commons, some adjustments were made in the Chancellor's proposals affecting beer duty and income tax. The whole parliamentary procedure, from introduction of the budget to the grant of Royal Assent, lasted only ten days. Nobody who mattered in any party disputed the view that the bulk of wartime expenses should be added to the National Debt and not met out of current taxation.

Lloyd George's second wartime budget, in May 1915, was influenced by a special wartime problem not directly connected with financial requirements. By the early part of 1915, there was much concern about increasing drunkenness, which was perceived not only as a social problem but as a serious threat to wartime production. The Government proposed, among other things, heavy taxation on alcoholic drinks. The duty on spirits would be doubled; high-gravity beer would be subjected to special taxation and the duty on wines would be quadrupled.

The reality of the problem of wartime drinking was not in doubt, but the Chancellor's proposals carried overtones of the old temperance debates and of party controversies which had been raging for 20 years and more. Unionists suspected that the Liberal Government was using wartime needs as an excuse to introduce measures which some of its members desired for quite different reasons. In the end, a compromise emerged. The proposed new taxes were dropped, but new legislation was introduced to control the production and sale of 'immature spirits', which were seen as the main cause of the spate of drunkenness.

This debate was a symptom of growing uneasiness on the part of opposition politicians. Several different issues were bound together; but it was clear that party politics were by no means dead. The upshot was another compromise. Later in May 1915, a Coalition Government was set up. Asquith remained Prime Minister, and the Liberals retained the lion's share of ministerial offices; but a number of Unionists, and several members of the Labour Party, entered the Government. One of the most remarkable changes was that Lloyd George left the Exchequer to head a new Ministry of Munitions. His successor was Reginald McKenna, another Liberal, but a man of far less charismatic character.

In the next few months, some Ministers began to show anxiety about the current level of expenditure, and, in particular, the level of borrowing. This concern was to some extent a reaction to the active campaign for military recruitment which was then in progress. McKenna, perhaps on the prompting of his Treasury advisers,[1] was worried about the financial consequences of withdrawing workers from the labour market, while Balfour advanced similar objections, which were countered with some heat by his Conservative colleague, Bonar Law.[2]

Whatever various politicians thought at that moment about possible reductions of military expenditure, there was a more persistent feeling that every effort must be made to cut down on all kinds of economic activity not directly relevant to prosecution of the war. McKenna's first budget, in September 1915, caught this mood.

The Chancellor proposed, and Parliament agreed, that existing taxation, both direct and indirect, should be raised substantially. The duties on tea, coffee, cocoa, sugar, tobacco and other consumer items were much increased, as also were duties on petrol and patent medicines. A new Excess Profits Duty of 50 per cent was introduced. Income Tax was raised by 40 per cent, although – as in Lloyd George's first wartime budget – the full effect was not immediately felt. Some other adjustments were made in both Income Tax and Super Tax, and the exemption limit for income tax was reduced from £160 to £130.

The feature of McKenna's budget which would have most lasting significance was what became known as the 'McKenna Duties' – charges of one-third *ad valorem*, which the Chancellor proposed to apply to miscellaneous imported items, including cars, motor cycles, clocks, watches, musical instruments, hats and plate glass.

The principle behind the McKenna Duties was to discourage wartime imports of non-essential items. But – like the drink taxes which Lloyd George had proposed in his spring budget – they attracted eager support from people who favoured them for different reasons from immediate requirements. This time, it was not the Temperance supporters who rejoiced, but Protectionists who saw them as a useful lever to achieve permanent changes in the taxation system: the first step towards a general system of tariffs, designed essentially to exclude imports rather than to raise revenue. Despite McKenna's hitherto impeccable Free Trade record, some Liberal back-benchers described them as 'the thin end of the wedge of Tariff Reform'. In the end, the proposed McKenna Duties were modified. The proposed duties on hats and plate glass were withdrawn, and concessions were made on several other particular items of taxation.

Like all other wartime budgets, McKenna's budget of 1915 also sought an increase in overall state revenue. The Chancellor's estimate of receipts on the basis of existing taxation was £272.1 million; the estimate after the changes which he proposed was £305 million. Actual receipts, however, were £336.8 million. This difference is not attributable to a buoyant economy, nor to overcaution on the part of the Chancellor, but rather to developing inflation. For almost a century before 1914, sound money had been a cardinal principle of all governments, but almost immediately the war began, that was thrown to the wind. The same pattern of receipts exceeding estimates by a large margin was observed for the remainder of the war.

McKenna's second budget, in the spring of 1916, proposed further large increases in duties on consumer goods. This time, there were other significant taxation changes as well. Income tax rose from 3 to 5 shillings in the pound – 25 per cent of taxed incomes.

In December 1916, a sort of palace revolution took place in the Government, as a result of which Asquith was replaced as Prime Minister by Lloyd George. Both the former Prime Minister and his closest associates, including McKenna, left office altogether, and many of them would never return. Lloyd George was able to form another three-party Coalition; but departure of many leading Liberals gave the Unionists a much larger part in the Government than hitherto. The new Chancellor was the Conservative Bonar Law.

In the second half of the war, taxation continued to rise. Duties on sugar, tobacco, matches and entertainments were increased. In 1918, there was a massive increase in duties on beer and spirits. In view of the reception which Lloyd George's proposals had received three years earlier, it is striking that these changes were proposed by a Conservative Chancellor.

At the same time, Income Tax was raised from 5 shillings in the pound to 6 (30 per cent).

Even before the fighting ended, the Coalition Government produced its first major measure of postwar reconstruction, the Education Act which was promoted by H.A.L. Fisher in 1918. The minimum school leaving age was raised to 14 in all cases, and the various exceptions which had previously existed ceased to apply. Secondary schools were to be expanded greatly, while free, or subsidised, places in them became widely available. When the Act came to be applied, however, there would be great variations in practice between different local authorities which were required to administer it. Expenses were to be shared between the State and local authorities. Education had cost the local ratepayers a little over £40 million a year at the end of the war; by 1939 it cost them over £100 million. In the same period, government spending on education and cognate matters rose from a little over £25 million to more than £60 million. The difference between these figures was partly the result of inflation, but there was a substantial increase in real terms as well.

The 1918 budget was, for practical purposes, the last budget of the war. The Armistice was signed on 11 November of that year. Although the peace treaties had not yet been concluded, and some warlike operations (notably the blockade of Germany) were continuing at the time of the 1919 budget, yet for practical purposes it was possible to stand back and assess the financial burden of the war.

Votes of Credit had been granted, from 7 August 1914 to 13 November 1918, to a total sum of £8,742 millions.[3] The total expenditure from the beginning of the financial year 1914–15 to the end of the financial year 1918–19 was about £9,593 million. These figures are not identical, but when allowance is made for the different periods covered, they are close enough. The average annual expenditure was therefore £1,918.6 million, compared with £197.5 million in 1913–14, an increase of nearly tenfold.

Against the enormous sum expended over the five financial years, tax revenue was about £2,391 million, and non-tax revenue about £342 million, totalling £2,733 million. Thus £6,860 million, or 71.5 per cent of the total, was met by borrowing. The National Debt, which had been about £650 million in March 1914, had been multiplied by a factor of more than ten. The annual interest on that debt, which had to be met from current taxation, was increased from £19.3 million to about £270 million. Debt interest alone was considerably greater than pre-1914 expenditure on all items combined.

As has been seen, the overall tax revenue in 1913–14 had been a little over £163 million. In 1918–19 it was over £784 million. To some extent, the difference may be attributed to wartime inflation. When the second figure is adjusted for the changed cost of living, it is brought down to £371 million in pre-war values; but even this represents more than double the burden.

The incidence of taxation according to income changed greatly. The old pattern, by which the very poor paid a higher proportion of their income in taxation than did the upper working class or lower middle class, was much less marked at the end of the war. By 1918–19, the poorest paid a shade under 10 per cent, and those earning £200 a year about 8 per cent. Thereafter the percentage rose steeply with increasing income, reaching a figure between 50 and 60 per cent for the very rich.

Both direct and indirect taxes had increased greatly during the war, but direct taxes had become a much higher proportion of the whole. In 1913–14, direct taxation had been 57.5 per cent; in the last financial year of the war it stood at 79.5 per cent.

This shift in taxation was linked with the increasing 'democratisation' of Income Tax. The total number of Income Tax payers in 1913–14 has been estimated at 1.13 million; by 1918–19 it stood at nearly 3.55 million. To some extent this may be explained by the reduction of the exemption limit from £160 to £130 in McKenna's budget of September 1915, and to the high wartime wages earned in civilian employment; but it was largely due to the falling value of money and the corresponding rise in nominal wages.

Almost immediately after the Armistice, Lloyd George's Coalition was remodelled. The new Government was, in effect, an uneasy alliance of Conservatives with a section of the Liberals. In December 1918, a General Election was held, which confirmed the Coalition in office.

As the war approached its conclusion, the Government correctly antici-pated that substantial unemployment would occur in the period between the onset of demobilisation and the time when substantially all ex-servicemen could be absorbed into industry. About the time of the Armistice, plans were introduced for a special donation to the unemployed; but a few months later there were more than one million claimants and complaints were being raised by members of the more comfortable classes that the cost was excessive.

Yet nobody seems to have anticipated the chronic mass unemployment of the inter-war years, and when the new problem first appeared at the beginning of the 1920s, heavy new taxation was required to deal with the resulting poverty. Poor relief, which fell on local government, was costing just under £15 million a year in 1919, and something closer to £35 million when Lloyd George's Coalition Government fell in 1922; while the central government's contribution to health, labour and insurance, which had been a little over £20 million a year at the end of the war, had reached more than £50 million by 1922.

After the General Election, the Government was again remodelled. Bonar Law, who was appointed Lord Privy Seal, became for practical purposes Lloyd George's second-in-command, and Austen Chamberlain moved to the Exchequer. This was a mark not only of increasing Conservative influence, but also of increasing influence for the old 'Tariff Reform' wing of the Conservatives.

After 1918, the wartime expedient of Votes of Credit was abandoned and proper itemisation of expenditure became possible. In his first budget of the new régime, in 1919, Austen Chamberlain attempted an estimate of what 'normal' peacetime requirements would eventually be, after the outstanding backlog of wartime expenses had been discharged.

The Chancellor contemplated a 'normal' expenditure of £766 million. Of this sum, £400 million – a pessimistic estimate, as it turned out – would be needed to meet debt charges, including the Sinking Fund. At the existing rate of taxation, revenue would yield £652 million towards requirements. And so, if something like a 'balanced budget' was to be produced, this would require levels of taxation even greater than those which had existed in wartime: a daunting prospect for any Chancellor.

There were further complications. In the first place, 'normal' conditions still did not exist, and a substantial period was bound to elapse before finances could settle on anything like an even keel. For practical purposes, that particular problem was resolved by allowing the National Debt to continue rising until 'normal' conditions returned.

Second, the Chancellor's personal convictions and family traditions were relevant to the construction of the budget. Resolution of some of these matters still lay in the future, but one received immediate attention in 1919. Austen Chamberlian shared his father's devotion to the idea of Imperial Preference and he proposed to advance this cause in two ways. In some cases, existing duties would be retained for foreign imports, but reduced for Empire imports; in a few cases, new duties would be imposed on foreign imports but not Empire imports.

The duty reductions on Empire goods would be of two main kinds. The McKenna Duties of 1915 were to be retained for foreign goods, but reduced by one-third for Empire goods; while the import duties on a large number of important items which had been taxed for many years would remain unchanged for foreign goods, but would be reduced by one-sixth for Empire goods. There would also be some reductions of duty on Empire wines. The main increase in duties proposed would be a surtax of 2s 6d in the pound per proof gallon on foreign spirits.

These various changes in duty, which may be attributed more to the Chancellor's sense of filial piety than anything else, would entail, overall, a loss of duty of about £3.3 million in a full year, and £2.5 million in the current financial year: a remarkable step to take at a time when, by common consent, further revenue was required. The emotional hangover from pre-war days was great and the proposed changes were debated with passion on both sides. In the end they passed into law as the Chancellor wished.

Other much greater taxation changes which Austen Chamberlian proposed were accepted with less fuss. Excess Profits Duty was reduced from 80 per cent to 40 per cent; but in most respects taxation was increased. Substantial increases were made in duties on beer and spirits. There was a large increase in Death Duties, and their scale became more steep. For estates valued at over £2 million, they produced a maximum of 40 per cent: double the previous top rate. And so, with an increase of £60 million on projected Inland Revenue, and nearly £49 million on Customs & Excise, the hypothetical 'normal' expenditure was nearly met.

Politics is full of paradoxes. Austen Chamberlain, the Conservative[4] Chancellor, was drastically eroding inherited wealth. He was also applying swingeing taxation on alcoholic drinks, which in other circumstances would have been greeted with huge delight by the Temperance lobby among the Liberals, and with dismay by the brewing interests which usually supported the Conservatives. As for the new Imperial Preference measures, they were built largely on the wartime duties introduced by McKenna, who had owed his tenure of the Exchequer more to his earlier reputation as a Free Trader than to anything else. But the overall effect of Chamberlains's Imperial Preference was not great in either the immediate or the long term, and both sides were probably disappointed by the undramatic upshot.

By the spring of 1920, it was at last possible to budget for a surplus for the first time since the war began. In most respects, taxation was either unaltered or increased. Duties on beer, spirits and wine were all raised further, and there would be an *ad valorem* duty on imported cigars. Stamp Duties and Super Tax were both revised, on the whole in an upward direction. Excess Profits Duty was raised again to 60 per cent, after the previous year's reduction.

The one significant reduction in taxation which Austen Chamberlain proposed was one whose significance was more symbolic than practical, and – as in the previous year – it was the symbolic change which attracted most attention. The Chancellor proposed to repeal the Land Value duties, which Lloyd George himself had introduced in 1909 and which had been at the centre of the great Budget debate.

It had never been Lloyd George's intention that these duties should be much more than an excuse for land valuation. As has been seen, he anticipated a revenue of only about £500,000 a year. If anything, this had proved something of an overestimate. The taxes had lingered during the decade which followed, but the revenue produced did not justify the costs of collection. Even the valuation had not worked in the way intended. Years later, Sir Edgar Harper, who had been Chief Valuer of the Board of Inland Revenue in 1910, gave a lucid explanation of what had gone wrong. Many unnecessary complications had been introduced into the valuation procedure, and the whole matter could have been conducted in a manner which was much less complicated, expensive and tedious – and also more accurate – if the Government had followed the ordinary procedure which valuers adopt.[5] Furthermore, the valuation was related to 1909 figures, which were wildly out of date by 1920.

On the face of it, Austen Chamberlain had a strong case for the view that taxation and valuation should both be scrapped. Criticism of the Chancellor's recommendations came, predictably, from the land taxers. Their real concern, however, was not to retain the 1909 valuation, but to conduct a new valuation on current figures. This possibility, however, was not included in the Chancellor's proposals, and – as parliamentary procedure operated – there was probably no way of debating that possibility except as a legislative proposal separate from the annual Finance Bill. So an unreal debate ensued, whose upshot was a foregone conclusion, and the predominantly Conservative House of Commons accepted the recommendations set before it.

11 Between the Wars

When Austen Chamberlain's Finance Bill received Royal Assent on 4 August 1920, it seemed that financial 'normality' had at last returned after six years of war and consequential disruption. The budget had been balanced; extraordinary wartime expenditure had ceased.

The new 'normality' was different from pre-war 'normality'. The annual sum demanded of the taxpayers was more than six times as great as it had been immediately before the war. The annual tax receipts had been £163 million 1913–14 and were £1,032 million in 1920–1. Correcting for the increased cost of living, the tax demanded was still about twice as great as the highest pre-war figure.

Of the total sum, 29 per cent, instead of less than 12 per cent, was now required to service the National Debt. Both direct and indirect taxation had increased, but direct taxation formed a substantially greater proportion of the whole than in pre-war days. In 1913–14, it had been 57.5 per cent, in 1921–2, when the wartime upsurge had abated, it stood at 62.7 per cent. After that date, it remained regularly well in excess of 60 per cent.

The principal items of direct taxation were Income Tax and Super Tax. The wartime surge had been followed by some abatement, but when relative stability returned, the figures were a good deal higher than they had been in pre-war days. In 1913–14, about 1.13 million people paid Income Tax; in 1920–1 about 3 million. Thereafter the numbers dropped considerably, but were never less than about 2.2 million. The standard rate of Income Tax, which had been 1s 2d in the pound (5.8 per cent) in 1913–14, reached 6 shillings (30 per cent) in the closing period of the war, and remained at that figure until the end of the tax year 1921–2. The 1919 increase in death duties signalled another permanent change in the pattern of 'normal' taxation.

But financial 'normality', however the term was understood, would not persist much longer. As has already been seen, nobody appears to have anticipated the chronic mass unemployment of the inter-war years, and when the new problem first appeared in the 1920s, heavy new taxation was required to deal with the resulting poverty. Poor relief, which fell on local government, was costing just under £15 million a year in 1919, and something closer to £35 million when Lloyd George's Coalition Government fell in 1922; while the central Government's contribution to health, labour and insurance, which had been a little over £20 million a year at the end of the war, had reached more than £50 million by 1922.

113

Unemployment was but one mark of a deeply troubled economy. It was matched by business failures and members of all classes became profoundly uneasy about the future. Radically different proposals for change in taxation policy were advocated increasingly by different people as possible ways of improving the situation. 'Soaking the rich' through high direct taxation; a revival of Protection; the taxation of land values as a major element, and perhaps even the only element, in the system of public revenue ... all these ideas, and many others, had their eager advocates, inside Parliament as well as outside it.

At the same time, political parties were being made and broken. The Coalition was coming under increasing criticism – from Liberals, from Conservatives and from the rapidly growing Labour Party. Almost any kind of political development seemed possible, and – whatever happened – taxation policy was likely to be deeply affected.

The United Kingdom itself, in the old sense of the term, was breaking apart, for the future relationship between Great Britain and Ireland lay in the balance. Irish taxation had been a bone of contention for many years. The Union of 1801 did not produce identical taxation for Britain and Ireland, although the UK Parliament set taxation for both countries. Thereafter, repeated complaints were heard from Ireland to the effect that taxation provisions of the Act of Union were being violated, or that Ireland was unfairly taxed, or both. As time went on, many pieces of special legislation were enacted for Ireland, dealing with matters as disparate as the relief of extreme poverty, the ownership of land and control of violent crime. Most of these measures involved more or less expenditure of public money, and therefore had implications for taxation.

From 1919 onwards, Irish disaffection turned to civil war. In the course of 1921–2, a sort of solution emerged. The six mainly Protestant counties of the north-east were to remain part of the United Kingdom, although they had acquired a subsidiary parliament of their own, with limited powers of taxation, The remaining 26 Irish counties were constituted as the Irish Free State, with its own government and taxation powers.

Agreement was reached between the UK government and the rebel Irish leaders on such financial problems as the division of the National Debt between the two countries and who was to pay for the many outstanding pensions, most particularly for war service. The agreement was disputed both in the United Kingdom Parliament and in the Irish Dáil, In the end, both accepted it: Parliament with large majorities in both Houses, the Dáil much more narrowly. Thereafter, Parliament abandoned all powers of taxation in the great bulk of Ireland. The link with Northern Ireland remained and the Province was usually a financial burden on Great Britain.

Early in 1921, Austen Chamberlain left the Exchequer and was replaced by a relatively unknown Conservative, Sir Robert Horne. The 1921 budget, which had been prepared by Horne but was actually introduced by his predecessor, resulted in the abolition of one wartime tax, the Excess Profits Duty. The Duty had been based on the idea of taxing the difference between wartime and pre-war profits. Excess Profits Duty had made good sense, both financially and politically, at a time when some firms were making large profits simply as a result of various quirks of the wartime economy. After the war, it had become increasingly difficult to assess and less and less realistic.

The few other tax reliefs which Horne introduced were of minor importance; but a couple of months later, the Government proposed further taxation changes of a more controversial nature, with different objects in mind. The Safeguarding of Industries Bill – commonly called the Key Industries Bill – proposed import duties on certain goods, with the avowed object of protecting domestic producers from foreign competition. The legislation was to last, in the first instance, for five years. On its face, it was a serious attack on the principle of Free Trade, although in practice the changes proposed were probably less drastic than eager contestants on either side contemplated.

A curious procedural point arose as the Key Industries Bill passed through Parliament, which had some constitutional importance. The House of Lords sought to amend the bill, slightly reducing its application. The Government declared that it was a 'Money Bill' within the meaning of the Parliament Act of 1911, and therefore not susceptible to amendment by the Lords, a view endorsed by the House of Commons.

There was much irony in the upshot. The Protectionist Austen Chamberlain, who had resisted reduction of the Lords' power in 1910–11, refuted the Lords' authority to interfere with the Bill. The Free Trader Asquith – who had been returned to the House of Commons in a sensational by-election a year earlier – took the same view, upholding the right of the Commons to impose whatever financial legislation it desired, even though he had strenuously resisted that legislation a few weeks earlier. In the end, the Lords withdrew their proposed amendments, and the Bill passed into law more or less as the Government had wished.

The Lloyd George Coalition ended abruptly in October 1922, when rank-and-file Conservatives rebelled against their own leaders within the Government. Bonar Law, whose health now seemed better, reluctantly set himself at the head of the revolt and soon became Prime Minister. Shortly afterwards, the Conservatives won a convincing overall majority at a General Election. The new Chancellor, Stanley Baldwin, inherited a large budget surplus in 1923, and was able to propose substantial tax reductions.

Significantly, the principal items affected were Income Tax and the tax on beer.

Very soon after this, Bonar Law's health finally collapsed and Baldwin became Prime Minister. Later in 1923, he announced his opinion that a return to Protection was necessary, but agreed to meet the challenge of a General Election on the question. After the Election, the Conservatives remained the largest single party, but the combined support of Labour and the Liberals, both of whom supported Free Trade, was substantially greater. Several weeks of political uncertainty followed. Eventually, in January 1924, Labour formed its first Government.

When Philip Snowden introduced the budget three months later, it was essentially a Free Trade budget rather than a Socialist budget. Like his Conservative predecessor, Snowden had the advantage of a substantial surplus. The McKenna Duties, which had long outlived their original purpose, but which had pleased the Protectionist majority in the previous two Governments, were abolished. The Chancellor was also able to secure large reductions in the duty on such items as sugar, tea and coffee.

Another General Election in the autumn of 1924 resulted in a large Conservative majority. Baldwin, who became Prime Minister for the second time, caused general astonishment by appointing Winston Churchill as Chancellor. Not only was a Protectionist Prime Minister giving the Exchequer to a man whose record had been as a Free Trader, but he was passing over senior men with long service in his own party in favour of a man who had fought as a Liberal candidate less than a year earlier. Churchill was to remain at the Exchequer until the Government fell in 1929.

The financial measures of the Conservative Government did not fully satisfy either Protectionists or Free Traders. In Churchill's 1925 budget, the McKenna Duties were restored, silk and hops were taxed and imperial preference was applied to a number of consumer items. Income Tax and Super Tax were reduced, but Death Duties were increased.

Taxation changes in the next few years were not dramatic. Some new items came within the range of taxation, notably betting, and taxes on several items were varied – some upwards, others downwards. The 'Key Industries' Duties of 1921 were renewed in 1926, this time for ten years, and several new items were brought within their range

Churchill's last budget, in 1929, included one feature to which enormous significance would have been attached a few decades earlier, but which by then was of relatively minor importance, The tea duty, which had persisted since the days of the first Elizabeth, was at last abolished. At one time, the duty on tea had represented a substantial element in the finances of a working-class family, but by 1929 remission of the tax represented a loss of State revenue just a little over £6 million, and probably had little effect in most households.

For most of the 1920s, people found it difficult to appreciate that mass unemployment was not just a temporary phenomenon which would soon disappear of its own accord. At the turn of the decade, however, some important legislation – by the Conservatives in 1929, by a Labour Government in 1930 – resulted in more radical changes in policy. The old Poor Law Unions disappeared and were replaced by new Public Assistance Committees. The burden of poor relief which fell on the local authority ratepayers was matched by a similar sum from the government.[1]

Financial policy of the later 1920s involved other changes which had a bearing on taxation. In 1925, the Minister of Health, Neville Chamberlain, half-brother of Austen, introduced important changes in the system of pensions. These were to become contributory, like National Insurance, with employers and workers paying in the ratio $2:1$. Pensions for widows and their children were introduced. The qualification age for the Old Age Pension was reduced from 70 to 65 and the old means qualification was removed.

There were also substantial changes in the system of local government finances. For many years, agricultural property had been assessed at only 25 per cent of its rateable value; in 1929 it was completely de-rated. At the same time industrial property was to be assessed at 25 per cent of its rateable value. These changes were met by State grants in relief of rates, thereby transferring the burden from local to national taxation.

Shortly after Churchill's Finance Bill of 1929 passed into law, a General Election was held. No party received an overall majority, but Labour had more MPs than either of the others and so formed the Government. In the autumn of the same year, the 'Wall Street crash' inaugurated the Great Depression. Thus the next few Budgets were drawn up under the shadow of highly adverse trading conditions, rapidly rising unemployment, business failure and general economic gloom. In such conditions, taxation revenue fell below expectations, while the demand for spending, particularly in connection with unemployment, rose rapidly.

For the first few months, the magnitude of the crisis was hardly perceived, and in his budget of April 1930 Snowden was concerned to meet the inevitable deficit by traditional means. Labour, like the Liberals, was disposed to favour direct rather than indirect taxation, and so the principal features were an increase in the standard rate of Income Tax from 4 shillings to 4s 6d (18.75p) in the pound, an increase in Surtax (as Super Tax was now called) and an increase in Death Duties. The only significant change in indirect taxation was an increase in the duty on beer.

It will be recalled that Snowden's 1924 budget had included repeal of the McKenna Duties, but Churchill had restored them in the following year. The Chancellor left the House of Commons in no doubt that he would have wished to repeat his earlier performance. Such was the financial position, however, that he reluctantly consented to retain them for their revenue-raising functions.

A year later, the economic position had worsened considerably. Unemployment, which stood at 10.4 per cent of the insured population in 1929 and 16.1 per cent in 1930, reached 21.3 per cent in 1931. By this time, many people were taking fright at the growing demand for unemployment benefit and the diminishing volume of contributions to the State insurance scheme which covered that benefit. In February of that year, a Committee chaired by Sir George May had been established to review the question of public expenditure: a Committee whose Report a few months later was to have dramatic effects.

So far as it concerned current expenditure and taxation, the budget of April 1931 was uneventful. Some adjustments were made in Income Tax, relating particularly to the timing of payments, and there was an increase in oil duty.

Much the most important feature of the budget in the Chancellor's mind was the proposal for land taxing. Snowden faced a problem similar in some ways to that which had confronted Lloyd George in 1909. The natural preliminary to a tax on land values was a general valuation of land; but a bill to value land would not rank as a 'Money Bill' and could therefore be rejected by the Lords. Snowden sought to overcome that difficulty by including valuation proposals in his budget, in which they were linked with proposals to impose a small tax on land values tn two years' time. The Finance Bill which contained these proposals encountered considerable difficulties in the Commons, but eventually passed into law.

Almost immediately, the Labour Government ran into even graver difficulties and it was soon replaced by a 'National Government' which, for a very brief space, looked like an all-party coalition. Soon, however, it came under Conservative domination, although, for various reasons, a number of Liberals and erstwhile members of the Labour Party remained in its ranks. But all members of the Government – indeed, so far as one can judge, nearly everybody else – agreed that immediate, dramatic and distasteful cuts in State spending were necessary to avert financial catastrophe. Today this attitude seems somewhat puzzling, when one reflects on the way in which vastly greater sums had been raised and spent during the 1914–18 war; yet the sincerity with which that view was held does not seem to be in doubt.

Philip Snowden remained Chancellor of the Exchequer in the National Government and his first task was to devise a budget involving substantial increases in taxation and reductions in expenditure. Parliament met early in September to hear and pass the Chancellor's proposals. Whatever uncertainties might exist about the long-term future of the Government and its component parties, it was tolerably certain that his main, immediate proposals would secure support from the Conservatives, the Liberals and a perceptible number of former members of the Labour Party. This would be enough to secure a comfortable majority in the House of Commons. In those circumstances, the Government could be confident of raising a sufficient loan on international markets to tide over the immediate crisis.

The budget which Snowden submitted in September 1931 does not look very different from the sort of budget which one might guess he would have proposed if the Labour Government had still been in place. The standard rate of Income Tax was to be raised from 4s 6d to 5 shillings in the pound (25 per cent). The system of allowances was revised to increase the number of Income Tax payers substantially – from about 2.2 million to about 4 million, according to one estimate.[2] Surtax rates would be raised. Indirect taxation would also be raised, but not in a way which would fall on absolute necessities of working-class people. The most impressive increase was in the tax on beer, but taxes on tobacco, hydrocarbon oils and entertainments also rose.

Snowden's budget, however, was linked with an Economy Bill proposed by the Prime Minister Ramsay MacDonald almost immediately afterwards, which bore clearer signs of the new political associations. There was to be a reduction of 10 per cent in most kinds of unemployment benefit and reduced payments for many other recipients of public salaries.

Inevitably, these economies, and most particularly the reduction in unemployment benefit, were widely criticised as measures falling most heavily on the poorest and most defenceless members of society. There was much in that criticism; but it must be remembered that one of the consequences of the Depression had been a substantial rise in the purchasing power of the pound.

Economies, additional taxation and an effective abandonment of the gold standard tided over the immediate financial crisis of 1931. The next important taxation changes turned on a chain of extraordinary political events. The original intention of the Prime Minister, and probably of all other participants in the National Government, had been that the administration should remain together until the crisis had been weathered, whereupon it should break up and a General Election should be held, in which the component political parties would make their several appeals to the electorate.

Matters followed a very different course. Soon the Conservatives perceived advantages in an early General Election, with the National Government intact. In the end, the pressure succeeded and a General Election was held on 27 October. The 1931 General Election produced an overall National Government majority of around 500: a figure wholly without precedent. Among Government supporters, Conservatives preponderated vastly over all others.

Soon after the election, Ministerial changes were announced. Ramsay MacDonald remained Prime Minister, but the general character of the Government became predominantly Conservative. Snowden, whose health was indifferent and who had not been a candidate at the election, was succeeded as Chancellor by Neville Chamberlain. The 'Liberal Nationals' – a group of erstwhile Liberals, most of whom were showing signs of losing their Free Trade faith – were brought into the government.

The Conservatives had been pressing for tariffs with growing insistence for some time, and were now in a position to get their way. The first step in that direction was taken almost immediately. It is surely ironical that the Minister set in charge of the legislation was Walter Runciman – who had a long reputation as a keen Free Trader. Importers correctly foresaw that the Government would soon impose tariffs on a large scale and sought to bring their goods into Britain while there was yet time. Runciman introduced the Abnormal Importations Bill, designed to authorise the Board of Trade to impose extra duties of up to 100 per cent on manufactured goods 'imported into the United Kingdom in abnormal quantities'. The measure, which was quickly passed, was to last only for six months and did not apply to Empire goods. A parallel bill applicable to horticultural products, and with effect for 12 months, was introduced by the Minister of Agriculture.

Early in 1932, the remodelled National Government encountered its first internal crisis. Even supporters of Protection were by no means clear as to what form a tariff policy might take. Were tariffs designed primarily to raise revenue, or were they designed to exclude foreign goods, which was clearly inconsistent? What should be the level of tariffs, and should they apply to all imports? In particular, should they apply to food, and should they apply to goods from the British Empire, as well as goods from foreign countries?

A sub-committee of the Cabinet sat over Christmas and set proposals before the Cabinet shortly afterwards. The upshot was largely predictable: the Protectionist members of the sub-committee supported a policy of tariffs; the Free Traders opposed it. Special provisions were to be made for Empire trade.

In Cabinet, the division between Free Traders and Protectionists persisted. As the Free Traders were in a minority, this division would in all ordinary circumstances have produced their resignation. At first both sides seem to have assumed that this must happen. But there were various reasons why most members of the Cabinet wished to avoid an early disruption of this kind. In the end, there was an 'agreement to differ'. The Free Traders would be authorised to speak and vote against the majority of their colleagues, without forfeiting their places in the administration.[3] Simple arithmetic, however, can have left nobody in doubt that the Protectionists would get their way.

The government proposals were introduced by Neville Chamberlain. There would be a general *ad valorem* duty of 10 per cent. One might well ask why this particular figure had been chosen for such a wide range of different goods. There appears to be no evidence that anyone ever saw it as a 'scientific' value, calculated by Treasury economists as an appropriate figure to meet the perceived needs of the 1930s. The origin of the figure seems to lie in the Chancellor's father's speech at Glasgow in October 1903, at the beginning of the ill-fated 'Tariff Reform' campaign, when he spoke tentatively about the desirability of 'a moderate duty on all foreign manufactured goods, not exceeding 10%'.

There were, however, some important exceptions to the general 10 per cent tariff. Items already subject to ordinary duties, like sugar and tobacco, or to the McKenna Duties and other similar levies, were excluded from further burdens. There would be a 'free list', which included grain, meat, fish of British taking and raw textile fibres, on which no duties would be charged. As an Imperial Economic Conference was planned for Ottawa in the summer, goods from the Dominions and India would be exempted, for the time being at least. Following the old idea of 'retaliation', the Board of Trade was authorised to impose a special duty of up to 100 per cent against goods from countries which discriminated against British goods. There would also be a special procedure for additional duties on luxuries.

Shortly afterwards, Neville Chamberlain introduced his first budget. The new tariff, he decided, would remove many of his anxieties; but a small gap remained. This he prepared to bridge by restoring the tax on tea which had been abolished three years earlier.

The Ottawa Conference which the Chancellor had foreshadowed resulted in a string of agreements. Britain was to continue her existing preference for Dominion goods and extend it to certain other items. The Dominions, in return, would either lower their tariffs against British goods or widen the preference margin in Britain's favour in other ways.

These agreements led to the departure of the Free Trade Ministers from the government. They were already under strong pressure from colleagues to withdraw, and the new agreements provided the occasion. The Liberal leader Sir Herbert Samuel, who was rather a good casuist, advanced two reasons why Ministers who had accepted the 'agreement to differ' in January could no longer remain in the Government. First, the new agreements were to last for five years and therefore Parliament could not amend the duties within that period; while the tariffs proposed in January had been unilateral and could be revoked at any time. Second – almost as an after-thought – 'the immediate object for which the National Government had been formed ... had been accomplished'.[4]

The 'real' Liberal members of the Government, and also Snowden, all resigned. At the first meeting of the Cabinet after their departure, MacDonald expressed some doubts as to whether the administration was still qualified to call itself a 'National Government'; but his colleagues reassured him.[5] For the time being the Free Traders continued to sit on the overcrowded government benches, but in 1933 they finally crossed into opposition.

The fiscal policy established in 1932 remained in place for the remainder of the National Government's life. Gradually, extreme slump conditions abated in Britain, as in other couritries. In 1934, Neville Chamberlain felt justified in reducing income tax to a more 'normal' figure of 4s 6d in the pound (22.5 per cent).

The same year witnessed another change, though it was really one of form rather than of substance. In his 1932 budget, Neville Chamberlain suspended the land value tax which Snowden had carried a year earlier, and which was due to take effect in the financial year 1933–4. There was pressure for the measure to be repealed altogether, but Baldwin resisted this, pointing out that Snowden's support had been of considerable value to the government at the recent General Election. Another attempt in the following year produced the same result, but in 1934 the land taxing legis-lation was repealed.

In 1935, MacDonald resigned and Baldwin became Prime Minister. Soon afterwards, a new General Election gave the National Government a reduced, but still enormous, majority.

By this time, new considerations of an international character were attracting an increasing measure of public attention. In the second half of the 1920s, international relations had been remarkably good. The arrival of the Great Depression, however, was immediately followed by the adoption of policies of economic nationalism in many countries – of which the British tariff legislation is but one example. Soon economic nationalism led to international disruption.

In February 1932, a Disarmament Conference met, which was attended by representatives of all important countries in the world. Almost immedi-ately, it ran into troubles of various kinds; but in October 1933 Germany

withdrew altogether, and – for practical purposes – the Conference collapsed. Failure to agree about disarmament was taken generally as a signal
for rearmament, and in the following year the British Government took its
first tentative steps in that direction. In the period which followed, rearmament was rapidly stepped up.

Rearmament was bound to have an important effect on taxation.
'Defence' spending, which had been in the range £100–115 million a year
since the middle 1920s, reached nearly £137 million in 1935–6 and £196
million in 1936–7. Taxation increases in Neville Chamberlain's 1936 budget acknowledged the need for a good deal more revenue to sustain rearmament. The standard rate of Income Tax was raised from 4s 6d in the
pound to 4s 9d (23.75 per cent), while the tax on tea was raised by 2d
a pound.

In the course of the 1930s, another significant change took place in the
pattern of taxation, for very different reasons. The legislation of 1891 had
provided that tithes should be paid not by a tenant but by a landowner. In
most places, this took the sting out of the tithe controversy, without greatly
altering the economic position of tenant, landowner or tithe-owner.

There were some places, however, where the friction continued, and
these were usually places where many farmers owned their own land.
After 1918, there had been radical changes in the pattern of rural land
ownership. Agricultural prices showed a general decline in real terms, and
in consequence farm rents also fell. Many landowners were pleased to sell
their land to tenants, who therefore became direct tithepayers. Agricultural
prices dropped, particularly during the Depression of the early 1930s. The
tariff policy of the National Government not only failed to help the farmers, but sometimes made their position worse, for they often had to bear
increased prices on their requirements, while their products were largely
unprotected.

In these conditions, tithes became a serious irritant. A new 'tithe war'
developed. Eventually, a Royal Commission was set up to examine the
matter, and its recommendations formed the basis of a bill introduced in
1936. Tithes were to be extinguished and tithe-owners would receive government stock, redeemable in 1996, in compensation. In the meantime, the
contribution of former tithepayers would be substantially less than the former tithes. Provision was made for payment out of public funds for such
purposes as maintenance of the fabric of cathedrals, provision of pensions
and payments to necessitous clergy. The bill had a stormy passage, and
was criticised both by staunch churchmen and by tithepayers; but in the
end it passed into law substantially unaltered.

12 The Second World War

The 1914 war came suddenly and the change in public finance was abrupt. The 1939 war, by contrast, cast long shadows before it and international relations had been deteriorating for a number of years. As a result, the transition from peacetime finance to war finance in Britain was less sharp, and significant changes had already taken place long before war was declared.

In February 1937, when Stanley Baldwin was still Prime Minister of the National Government and Nazi Germany had not yet crossed any international frontier,[1] the Defence Loans Bill was set before the House of Commons. This proposed that the Treasury should be authorised to raise up to £400 million over the next five years, by way of loans, for 'defence' purposes. Neville Chamberlain, Chancellor of the Exchequer, argued that this sum would not injure national credit, while to raise the money by taxation would set a 'crushing burden' on the taxpayer and throw back the trade revival. The bill encountered predictable Opposition criticism, but passed into law swiftly and without much difficulty.

Here was a radical change in financial policy. For well over a century, peacetime rearmament had always been financed out of taxation. As a general rule, the National Debt was reduced year by year in peacetime, and when that debt increased – as in the early 1930s – it was because of some special economic emergency. The current decision clearly implied that the country had entered a period of great crisis, which must soon be resolved either by a general *détente* or by war.

What followed thereafter confirmed this view. The budget of April 1937 was presented as a 'balanced' budget, but really something like £80 million was to be drawn from the new Defence Loan. The Chancellor's proposals included a rise in income tax to 5 shillings in the pound (25 per cent), but they also included new taxation proposals which excited a much greater political furore. A tax known as the National Defence Contribution (NDC) was proposed, which was to be levied on increased profits of industry, trade or business. The thinking behind the NDC was that these increases were largely related to rearmament spending, even when they occurred in firms which were not directly involved in armaments.

The main protests against the NDC came from the Government's own supporters. In the end, a face-saving compromise was produced. The NDC was remodelled as a straightforward tax on profits in excess of £2,000, levied at the rate of 4 per cent on individuals and 5 per cent on companies In this new form, it was accepted by Parliament.

Soon after Neville Chamberlain introduced his 1937 budget, Baldwin retired from the premiership and Chamberlain succeeded him. By the time that the new Chancellor, Sir John Simon, introduced his first budget, in April 1938, Germany had already occupied Austria and had started to exert that pressure on Czechoslovakia which would lead to the 'Munich' crisis in the early autumn. The possibility – indeed, the probability – of a major war involving Britain was now considerable and most politicians of all parties were willing to accept major increases in spending on the fighting services, which were budgeted at £55 millions more than in the previous year.

Inevitably, taxation rose. The standard rate of Income Tax was increased from 5 shillings to 5s 6d (27.5 per cent) – the highest level since 1922. The Petrol Tax was also increased, as was the tax on tea. Borrowing would again take place on a substantial scale; the Chancellor calculated that £90 million would be borrowed under provisions of the Defence Loans Act.

The international situation continued to deteriorate. The Munich settlement of September 1938 was not followed by the general 'appeasement' which the Prime Minister had hoped to see. Britain soon stepped up her rearmament programme. Within six months, Germany smashed the remains of Czechoslovakia. Chamberlain himself acknowledged that 'appeasement' was at an end. On 31 March 1939, Britain issued the so-called 'guarantee' to Poland, which was widely seen as a probable *casus belli* in the near future.

During this period of international commotion, a second Defence Loans Act, doubling the sum which might be borrowed for defence purposes, passed into law with scant comment. Simon's second budget, on 25 April 1939, planned for defence spending at £580 million – more than five times the figure which had been normal down to the middle of the decade. Of that sum, £350 million would be raised by borrowing. This estimate, the Chancellor warned Parliament, did not take account of recent commitments, which he reckoned would cost not less than £50 million.

As a mild concession to orthodox finance, Simon proposed to raise £20 million by increased taxation. This time, Income Tax was not affected, but Surtax and Death Duties were both raised. Taxes on cars, tobacco and foreign sugar were increased to a small extent. These increases, however, must be seen mainly as a sort of warning to the public that war might be coming soon, rather than an important source of public finance.

In June, a new tax was announced, not very different in principle from the original proposal for the National Defence Contribution of the previous year. An 'Armaments Profits Duty' was to apply to excessive armaments profits, at the rate of 60 per cent. This measure again was essentially symbolic in character – in this case, the mark of a determination to curtail personal gain which derived from national need. It passed into law without difficulty, but could hardly prove a major source of revenue.

On 1 September 1939, German troops entered Poland. On the same day, the Treasury was authorised to borrow a further £500 million charged against the National Debt: a Vote of Credit for a similar sum was also authorised. Thereafter, the Treasury was enabled to borrow as it required, while Votes of Credit were granted every few months.

The British declaration of war on 3 September 1939 was followed swiftly by an 'emergency' budget. This was a good deal more drastic than Simon's earlier budgets. The standard rate of Income Tax was raised from 5s 6d in the pound to 7 shillings (35 per cent): a figure without precedent, even in the 1914 war. Various allowances were reduced in scope. There were parallel increases in Surtax and Death Duties. Taxes on most kinds of alcoholic drinks were increased substantially, as also were duties on tobacco and sugar. The recent Armaments Profits Duty was to be merged in an Excess Profits Tax of 60 per cent, which would apply to all trades which profited from the war.

The new taxation may not have contributed much to the cost of war, but the psychology was excellent and there was little complaint. Everybody was seen to be paying something towards the national cause; nobody was suffering to a ruinous extent; and those who profited financially from the conflict were to be mulcted of most of their gains. On this occasion, as on others before and since, taxpayers were willing to pay sums which represented a perceptible erosion of their living standards, provided that other people were seen to be doing the same and the position of a particular taxpayer in the social hierarchy was not disturbed.

Simon's fourth and last budget, in April 1940, only altered taxation to a small extent. Income Tax was raised to 7s 6d (37.5 per cent), while allowances were somewhat curtailed. Rather more duty was charged on familiar items of indirect taxation like alcoholic drinks and tobacco. Simon recommended a new kind of sales tax – what eventually became known as Purchase Tax – but indicated that this would require special legislation at a later date.

If Simon had struck the right note in September 1939, he gravely miscalculated the national mood in April 1940. His taxation proposals were widely seen as not drastic enough to meet current needs, while the projected sales tax came under criticism as a burden which would fall particularly heavily on the poor. In these attacks one may perceive preliminary rumblings of the political explosion which would destroy Chamberlain's government a few weeks later.

On 10 May 1940, Winston Churchill emerged as Prime Minister of a truly all-Party Coalition. Simon had been one of the less popular members of the old administration and was removed to the more dignified and more lucrative, but also less powerful, office of Lord Chancellor. Sir Kingsley Wood, a Conservative who was well regarded by his erstwhile political opponents, became Chancellor of the Exchequer.

For the remainder of the war, taxation had to be acceptable to all parties in the Coalition. Several important changes were made at different points in the war. These changes were often introduced for psychological reasons – to stimulate wartime morale – as well as strictly economic reasons. Old taxes were changed and new taxes were introduced.

Income Tax had been a very important element in national taxation long before 1939. In the last years of peace, Income Tax and Surtax represented about 40 per cent of taxation income. Yet, right down to the early period of the war, Income Tax still fell mainly on people in the lower middle class and above. In the course of the war, civilian incomes rose, most particularly those of manual workers. By 1943, there were some 10 million Income Tax payers, and a great many of these were manual workers.

In the first period of the war, the standard rate of Income Tax rose rapidly, reaching 10 shillings in the pound (50 per cent) in 1941. Surtax increased as well. By 1942, the combined effect of Income Tax and Surtax in the very highest taxation brackets was a levy of 19s 6d in the pound, or 97.5 per cent. This, of course, affected very few people; but taxpayers with much lower incomes than that were coming to the view that there was little point in increasing their earnings, when a huge proportion of any increment would disappear in taxation. Thus any further increases in the standard rate of Income Tax were likely to prove damaging from the point of view of the Chancellor of the Exchequer, and even more so from the point of view of wartime productivity. Different kinds of variations in Income Tax were, however, possible.

An important innovation was introduced in the 1941 budget, which would cause much dispute long after the war. Allowances for earned incomes and personal allowances were curtailed substantially; but the difference between the old rate of personal or earned income allowance and the new would be counted in the taxpayer's favour to provide what became known as Postwar Credits. These Postwar Credits would become redeemable at an unstated date after the war. A similar procedure would apply to 20 per cent of the Excess Profits Tax.

Another change affected the manner in which the tax was collected. Before the war, Income Tax had been collected annually. This had worked more or less satisfactorily at a time when people paying Income Tax were, for the most part, sufficiently affluent and sufficiently familiar with financial management to budget ahead. But in pre-war days, working-class incomes had usually been so low that little long-term budgeting was possible. Now that millions of workers came within the range of Income Tax, many difficulties were raised for taxpayers and tax collectors alike.

After the 1943 budget debates, a working party was set up to consider the practicality of a 'pay-as-you-earn' (PAYE) system. The conclusions were favourable and Sir Kingsley Wood was due to make an important announcement on the subject on 20 September, but he died unexpectedly on the same day. The new scheme was announced a couple of days later and came into operation at the beginning of the following tax year. It proved a considerable success.

It was still possible to increase the burden of indirect taxes with less adverse effects on productivity than increases in direct taxes, and most wartime budgets recorded additions to the burdens on traditional items like alcohol, tobacco and entertainments. An important change in indirect taxation was the introduction of Purchase Tax, which Simon had foreshadowed in April 1940, and which appeared in a concrete form in Sir Kingsley Wood's first budget three months later. It would be charged at the rate of one-third on the wholesale price of what might roughly be called 'luxury' goods and it was calculated that this would entail about 24 per cent addition to retail prices. Non-luxury goods would be charged at one-sixth of wholesale prices, or about 12 per cent of retail prices. There would be complete exemption for food and drink, for services like water, fuel, electricity and gas, for children's clothing and for some goods which were already subject to high duties.

The principle behind Purchase Tax was not just to achieve the ordinary purposes of contemporary taxation – to collect money for wartime needs and to encourage a certain feeling that belts were being tightened for the national cause. There was also a growing concern at the government level to ensure that the rising wages which many civilians were experiencing as a result of the war did not produce too strong a demand for non-essential consumer goods, and did not lead to the dangerous inflation which had marked the 1914 war. Thereafter, Purchase Tax was rapidly increased, and by 1943 the rate on luxury and semi-luxury goods rose to 100 per cent of wholesale prices.

In the course of the Second World War, a sea-change took place in both public and official attitudes towards welfare and education: two major items of expenditure, which were bound to exert a great effect on future taxation. No doubt many factors were at work in producing that change, and this is not the place to analyse their respective contributions.

In December 1942, the Report *Social Insurance and Allied Services*, appeared. It had been produced by a group of civil servants, headed by Sir William Beveridge. The 'Beveridge Report' attracted immediate and widespread attention, not least among members of the armed forces. On its face, it was not dangerously radical and proposed little more than a unification, and some extension, of existing systems of contributions and payments for insurance against sickness, unemployment and various other vicissitudes.

Unsuccessful attempts were made to persuade the Coalition Government to present a united front in support of the Beveridge schemes. However, there were abundant indications before the war ended that all parties had been deeply influenced by the essential ideas of the Report and would take steps towards implementation if the opportunity presented itself.

Although there was no agreed policy on the Beveridge schemes, the wartime Coalition Government did undertake some major advances in the field of education, which took effect under the 'Butler Act' of 1944. The Act's main provisions could not, by the nature of things, come into immediate effect, but were brought into operation in the next few years. The school leaving age was to be raised from 14 to 15, and secondary education was to become universal. Between 1941 and 1948, local government spending on education doubled, while State spending increased nearly threefold. The overall cost, which had been £93 million in 1943, was £210 million five years later.

In the period of the wartime Coalition, two other important 'welfare' measures were proposed, which did not actually become law until after the government left office. Family Allowances were introduced, at the rate of 5 shillings (25p) a week for second and subsequent children. There was also legislation establishing a State scheme of insurance for industrial injuries. This was essentially similar in structure to the existing National Insurance scheme. An insurance fund was to be set up, to which contributions were made by employers, employees and the State, and from which employees sustaining industrial injuries would be entitled to draw benefit.

As in earlier wars, the Government allowed the National Debt to rise sharply, thus setting a large part of the burden of wartime expenditure on taxpayers of the future. Initially, this increase in the debt burden was achieved by traditional methods of raising money on the market. This became more difficult as the war advanced, but early in 1941, the United States inaugurated the system of 'Lease-Lend', which enabled Britain to acquire goods there on a huge scale and facilitated a massive, and continuing, increase in the National Debt.

In the middle period of the war, money was raised on a large scale by the even more damaging means of selling foreign investments. In his 1942 budget, Kingsley Wood foreshadowed that he proposed to raise £786 million in this manner, and the process was continued thereafter. Long before the war was over, it was therefore predictable that Britain's worldwide influence would be greatly reduced in the aftermath.

The rise in the National Debt was massive. In 1936, it stood at £7,784 million; by 1947 it had reached £25,631 million and the annual service charge was in excess of £500 million. In spite of these figures, the Government had been considerably more cautious in borrowing to finance wartime requirements than in the 1914 war. In his 1945 budget statement, delivered a very few weeks before the end of the European war, Sir Kingsley Wood's successor, Sir John Anderson, claimed that 49 per cent of expenditure throughout the conflict had been met by taxation, while in the most recent year, 1944–5, the proportion had been 53 per cent. By contrast it will be recalled that 71.5 per cent of the total cost of the earlier war had been met by borrowing.

The European war ended in May 1945, the Far Eastern war in August. Between those two dates, a General Election was held and resulted in the return of a Labour Government with a large majority.

The new Chancellor, Hugh Dalton, introduced a Supplementary Budget in October 1945. In many respects, this continued wartime practice, for emergency spending had not ceased. Wartime devices like massive and continuing increases to the National Debt, subsidies for foodstuffs in order to stabilise the cost of living and the use of Votes of Credit continued.

Some abatements of taxation were introduced in the budget, but most of these did not take immediate effect and were postponed until the end of the calendar year, or the end of the financial year. The standard rate of income tax would be reduced from 10 shillings in the pound to 9 (45 per cent), and there would be further reductions at the lower end of the scale. The rules governing personal allowances would be relaxed and Postwar Credits would cease to be given. Surtax would be increased in the upper ranges, so that at the very highest levels the combined incidence of Income Tax and Surtax would remain at 19s 6d in the pound (97.5 per cent). Excess Profits Tax would be reduced from 100 per cent to 60 per cent.

In his budget of April 1946, Dalton was able to move closer to normal financial practice. Votes of Credit were to cease and there would be specific votes for the fighting services. Tax changes were slight, the most important being a small increase in the earned income allowance.

Not until April 1947 was it possible to return to balanced budgeting. Estimated annual expenditure, which had peaked at just under £6,000 million at the time of the 1944 budget, had been reduced year by year. For 1947–8, it was down to £3,181 million, and was exceeded by anticipated revenue. Thus it was possible to grant further reliefs on Income Tax, although the standard rate was unchanged, and those reliefs were to a measure offset by an increase in the Tobacco Tax.

The 1939–45 war, like other wars, left a permanent burden on the tax-payers. The long-term effects of war continued for many years; some are still with us to this day. National taxation, in a rather narrow sense of the noun, had totalled around £900 million at the outbreak of war; by 1947 it was close to £3,500 million. Correction must be made for changes in the cost of living.[2] In 1937, gross government income was 19.7 per cent of national income, in 1947 it was 41.7 per cent.

Other considerations also played a large part in doubling the taxpayers' real burden. 'Defence' costs had increased enormously, and after the war they did not subside to anything like the prewar level, whether in nominal money terms or in real terms. In 1937, just before the Defence Loans Act took effect, they had totalled £186 million, which was 20.9 per cent of gross government expenditure and 4.1 per cent of national income. In 1947, when the decision to abandon Votes of Credit makes it possible again to derive a clear picture of how public money was allocated, 'defence' spending totalled £1,653 million, which was 39.4 per cent of gross government expenditure and over 9.4 per cent of national income.

13 Postwar Taxation

War expenditure did not abate as rapidly after 1945 as it had done after 1918. The reduction which did take place was to a substantial extent countered by increased spending on welfare. The most important measures were the National Insurance Act and the National Health Act, both of which were carried in 1946, but did not take full effect for a considerable time. Both were contentious and sharply debated in Parliament; but both had their origins in the great change of public attitudes towards welfare which developed in the middle period of the war and which influenced policies in all parties. Thus the debate concerned the form which the measures should take, not the principle that major welfare legislation was required.

The National Insurance Act streamlined, and greatly extended, the provisions of earlier legislation. Many of the provisions of the Act may be regarded as developments of existing law and practice; but there was also a major innovation. In addition to payments out of the fund, which were linked to the insurance scheme, all citizens would henceforth be entitled to National Assistance in case of special need – notably, for unemployment which was not covered by insurance, or which exceeded the benefit period.

Thus the Act introduced the principle of a 'safety net', setting minimum standards below which nobody would be allowed to fall. The contributory principle, which had been introduced in the legislation of 1911, remained in force. All parties accepted the principle of Full Employment – that is, that it should be a major feature of economic policy to ensure that there were more jobs available than people looking for jobs. Thus payments to unemployed workers would not impose a very severe burden on the general taxpayer for many years to come.

The National Health Service was supported by taxation. The Act provided a universal, free health service, charged against State funds. This did not exclude the right of either patients or practitioners to make other arrangements if they preferred. The Act's provisions covered medical and hospital care, and dispensing of medical prescriptions. The Act also provided for considerable structural changes in the hospital services and a system of state payment for medical practitioners.

As in the aftermath of the First World War, both government expenditure and taxation settled to fairly level rates within a few years of the end of the fighting.[1] In the financial years from 1947–8 to 1950–1, taxation receipts of the state were around £4,000 million a year. Of that sum, something between £1,420 million and £1,630 million, or between 36 per cent and 41 per cent of the total, were collected from customs and excise. The major direct taxes, of which Income Tax was by far the most important, yielded between £1,280 million and £1,560 million, or between 33 per cent and 40 per cent of the total. The yield of Profits Tax, at a little under £400 million a year, was substantially less than it had been in the closing years of the war.

The various nationalisation measures introduced by the Labour Government had little effect on the pattern of state expenditure and taxation. The practice was to replace existing stocks and shares by new fixed-interest stock. Payment of interest on this stock was a duty of the new corporations which were set up to control the nationalised industries.[2]

One change introduced in this period was of considerable historical interest, but of little practical importance. Although taxpayers had had the opportunity of commuting their liability under the eighteenth-century 'Land Tax' ever since the days of Pitt, a considerable number of people had not done so nearly a century and a half later. Legislation provided for compulsory redemption of liability for this archaic tax from April 1950 onwards, at a rate of 25 times the annual charge, whenever the property changed hands, whether through death, sale or for other reasons.

Early postwar years were marked by the very rapid development of a 'Cold War' climate. Diplomatic relations between Britain and the United States on one side and the Soviet Union on the other, became increasingly icy. Thus the anticipated 'peace bonus' was only partially realised after 1945, and expenditure on defence remained at a high level.

In the middle of 1950, war broke out in Korea. The conflict was followed swiftly by United Nations intervention, in which Britain participated. The Korean War represented a further deterioration in an international climate which was already bad, and many people recognised a serious risk of general war soon developing. The Government inaugurated a programme of substantial rearmament. The Economic Survey for 1951 forecast an increase of £375 million in defence spending over the previous year,[3] which represented an increase on all state expenditure of about 8 per cent.

In April 1951, the perceived need for rearmament led to substantial changes in both taxation and welfare benefits. Income Tax rose from 9 shillings in the pound to 9s 6d (47.5 per cent). Profits Tax, Purchase Tax, Petrol Tax and Entertainments Tax were all increased. More significantly, charges were introduced for spectacles and false teeth – the first incursion into the principle of a universal free health service. This produced Ministerial resignations shortly afterwards.

As the Labour Government had sustained many losses at the General Election of 1950, these defections probably weakened it to a fatal extent. The next General Election, in October 1951, gave the Conservatives a small overall majority and Winston Churchill became Prime Minister for the second time. Few people guessed it, but Britain had entered a period of remarkable consensus on domestic political and economic questions, which would last – with a few spectacular but short-lived interruptions – for more than a quarter of a century.

Public expenditure and consequential taxation continued on an even keel. The broad outlines of the welfare state which had been established in the 1940s were not questioned. Nobody who mattered denied the merits of full employment, at least in public. The great recent increase in military expenditure soon abated, for the Korean War settled on a line of stalemate in 1951, and – with the death of Stalin in 1953 – the threat of a Third World War gradually receded. Changes of party of government in 1964, in 1970 and in 1974, appear to have exerted remarkably little effect on the general pattern of events.

About half way through the period of 'consensus', some radical changes in taxation began to be introduced, and further changes continued to be made under both Labour and Conservative Governments. Some of the changes would prove short-lived, while others have persisted to the present.

The first spate of taxation changes arose under a Labour Government, and took effect through the budgets of 1965 and 1966. Two of these changes were of considerable importance. A new Capital Gains Tax was designed to collect 30 per cent of gains realised on assets – with some notable exceptions, including owner-occupied houses and life insurance policies. The Selective Employment Tax (SET) was a more complicated tax, designed partly as a revenue-raising device, partly to deflect labour from service industries to manufacturing industries, and partly as a 'payroll tax' to control what was popularly called 'over-full employment'. All employers would be required to pay a tax of 25 shillings (£1.25) a week for each adult male employee, and smaller sums for women and young people. The tax would be refunded to manufacturing industry, with a bonus on top; while it would be refunded to certain other kinds of industry without a bonus.

By contrast, the new Corporation Tax was designed as essentially a streamlining operation, or a belated recognition of the enormous part played by corporate bodies in modern life. Instead of corporations paying both Income Tax and Profits Tax, the revenue would be collected in the form of a consolidated tax. Thus, figures for overall Income Tax receipts before and after the Corporation Tax came into effect are not exactly comparable.

The second spate of taxation changes arose in the early 1970s, under a Conservative administration. It was largely related to the British decision to join the European Economic Community (EEC), which took effect at the beginning of 1973. Some of the changes anticipated the new economic and political relationship with the Western European countries, but took place at a time when the Conservative Government of Edward Heath was visibly determined to bring it about.

SET was halved in 1971 and abolished two years later, and Purchase Tax was also phased out. At the same time, a new tax, the value added tax (VAT) was introduced. VAT, which was favoured by the EEC, resembled purchase tax to some extent, but it involved taxation on services as well as goods and was more widespread in its application – though some commodities, including food, books and newspapers, were exempt. Various adjustments were made to existing revenue duties to accommodate VAT. The initial rate of VAT was 10 per cent but this was soon changed.

The end of one famous old tax was signalled in 1973. Surtax, formerly Super Tax, had long been for practical purposes an instalment of Income Tax, but was subject to different rules.[4] A unified system of personal taxation came into existence, covering incomes at all levels; so the distinction between Surtax and Income Tax was no longer necessary.

These changes in taxation pattern which the Conservatives had introduced were not reversed when a Labour Government took office in early 1974. In the first few years, however, there were considerable fluctuations in the rate of VAT and at times different items were charged at very different rates. However, the process of introducing important new taxes continued without abatement.

The Capital Transfer Tax, which was introduced in Denis Healey's budget of March 1974, was a competely different kind of tax from the Capital Gains Tax introduced a few years earlier and which was still in force. The similarity of name must have caused considerable confusion. The new Capital Transfer Tax was designed to extend Estate Duties – formerly Death Duties – to cover gifts from living donors, which in the past had sometimes been used to avoid tax liability. In the original form of the tax, lifetime gifts over £15,000, with a few exceptions, were to be taxed in a similar way to Estate Duties. A glance at receipts over the next few years does not suggest that the change made very much difference to the tax yield.

In the same 1974 budget, a quite new tax was foreshadowed, although it did not take effect until 1976. This was the Development Land Tax. The principle behind the tax was to bring land which was already available for development into use, by imposing a flat rate tax on development values realised from land. When the Government's principles eventually took leg-islative form, there were various exceptions and reductions of rate for land of limited value. The revenue collected was not great – £26.3 million in 1979–80 – but the object of the tax had been to bring land into use rather than to collect revenue. How far it succeeded in that object will call for later consideration.

A tax which would eventually produce a far greater yield appeared in 1975: the Petroleum Revenue Tax (PRT). Submarine reserves of oil and natural gas had been studied for some years, but their exploitation received a great impetus after the massive increase in world oil prices which took place in 1973, for there was growing uncertainty about the reliability of supplies from traditional Middle Eastern sources. The new PRT was first levied at the rate of 45 per cent on North Sea oil profits. Thenceforth, rev-enue was collected from this source under three separate heads: royalties; Corporation Tax; and the new PRT. The PRT yield first became substantial in 1978–9, when it produced around £183 million. Thereafter, the yield increased enormously, as will later be seen.

It is not easy to make an exact comparison of the burdens falling on taxpayers at different stages in the 1950s, 1960s and 1970s, for two main reasons. Imposition of new taxes sometimes meant that the incidence of old taxes was reduced, sometimes that they were abolished entirely, without necessarily making much difference to the taxpayers on whom they had been imposed. Thus, the revenue drawn from Income Tax was reduced when Corporation Tax was introduced, but was increased when Surtax was gradually abolished. VAT replaced Purchase Tax, but it also applied to things which had never been subject to Purchase Tax. The Capital Transfer Tax was similar to the old Estate Duties, but not identical, and so on. With some taxes, notably Income Tax, exemptions and the rates at which differ-ent taxation rates applied, changed considerably – almost from year to year.

The gross taxation income of the State was just under £4,000 million in the financial year ending 1951. Thereafter it rose, and continued to rise steeply, reaching no less than £43,088 million in the year ending 1979. Thus, over 28 years, the taxation yield multiplied more than tenfold. Receipts of local authorities from rates increased even more rapidly – growing from a little over £300 million in 1951 to more than £5,000 million in 1979.

The increase in taxation receipts may be attributed in some measure to the need to meet a real increase in spending by public authorities; but by far the most important cause was the inflationary policies of successive gov-ernments, Conservative and Labour alike. One study[5] showed that in 1950 the pound still retained 98 per cent of its purchasing power of 30 years earlier; but by 1980 its value was only 13.1 per cent of the 1920 value.

Social changes also make comparisons difficult. There was a general increase in living standards throughout the period, though the rate of increase fluctuated. This meant that people who had once been too poor to be liable for some kinds of taxes, like Income Tax and taxes on semi-luxury goods, now came within their range.

Taxed items like cars are obvious examples, but in such cases other factors were at work as well as a general increase in affluence. Before the war, many people who could have afforded cars did not feel the need to buy them; but by the later 1960s a car became seen as virtually a necessity for families with quite modest incomes. At the outbreak of war in 1939, just over 2 million private cars were in use. The number did not reach 2.5 million until 1952, but it passed 10 million in 1967, and 15 million in 1980. The revenue from motor vehicle duties in 1950–1 was £61.4 million, or rather less than 1.5 per cent of the gross income of the State. The vast increase in car numbers produced far less effect on taxation patterns than might have been expected. By 1979–80 the revenue was £1,148.9 million, which was only a shade over 2.1 per cent of overall State income.

With cars, and even more so with other taxed items like television sets, technological improvements made them relatively cheaper and also more useful, and this brought them into the hands of far more people than before. Other changes were exerting a large effect on living standards and – indirectly – on taxation patterns. In particular, more women were taking paid employment, and more young people were undertaking full-time studies.

With such reservations, it is possible to look at changes in taxation burdens during the long period of 'consensus politics'.

There was a substantial increase in taxation revenue, in real as well as money terms. An analysis presented by the Chancellor of the Exchequer in 1983[6] showed that the burden of central government taxes had increased by more than 50 per cent in real terms between 1963–4 and 1978–9, while the burden of local government rates had grown by almost the same amount. Over the 15-year period, the total of National Insurance contributions had more than doubled. Most of the increase had fallen on employers, but the extra burden on employees was also considerable.[7]

Over the same period, there was also a substantial shift in the proportions of different kinds of taxes, with direct taxation constituting a growing proportion of the whole. Income Tax, Surtax and Corporation Tax together had formed 39.9 per cent of the central government tax burden in 1963–4, 50.4 per cent in 1978–9. The proportion of taxes on expenditure declined from 45.7 per cent in 1963–4 to 36.9 per cent in 1978–9.

In spite of the general shift towards direct rather than indirect taxation, the standard rate – later known as the basic rate – of Income Tax declined substantially. It stood at 9s 6d in the pound (47.5 per cent) in 1951–2 and 1952–3, after which it was reduced in stages to 7s 9d (38.75 per cent), at which level it stood from 1959–60 to 1964–5. It was then increased to 8s 3d (41.25 per cent), after which it dropped, in two stages, to 30 per cent in 1973–4. Thereafter it fluctuated at levels from 30 per cent to 35 per cent during the remainder of the 1970s.

The last administration of the 'consensus' period was the Labour Government of 1974–9, under the premiership first of Harold Wilson and later of James Callaghan. This period witnessed the gradual collapse of full employment. On the assumption that an unemployment level of about 2.5 per cent was one at which the number of job vacancies corresponded roughly with the number of people seeking work, the United Kingdom departed from full employment in 1975. In that year, too, the number of registered unemployed people began regularly to exceed one million. Thereafter, the figure remained above a million, usually corresponding with 4 per cent of the labour force, for the remaining period of the Government's life.[8]

14 The Age of Confrontation

The formation of Margaret Thatcher's Conservative Government in May 1979 was followed by a substantial change in taxation policy, and the general thrust of the new administration was as different from Conservative Governments of the 'consensus' period as it was from Labour Governments. Margaret Thatcher's record leaves no doubt that she was deeply disturbed by what she saw as the failure of previous Conservative Governments to reverse the socialistic measures of Labour administrations and was determined to act differently.[1] Perhaps the most remarkable feature of the new Government was its disposition to allow unemployment, already high when it took office, to rise rapidly, evidently regarding this as necessary in order to attain its economic objectives.

There was an immediate change in the pattern of taxation. The new Chancellor of the Exchequer, Sir Geoffrey Howe, had a general reputation for caution, but his first budget, introduced in June 1979, made some very important departures from previous policies. The Government was particularly anxious to reduce Income Tax. The standard rate was brought down from 33 per cent to 30 per cent, the top rate from 83 per cent to 60 per cent. These changes were accompanied by an increase in VAT, which had previously stood at 8 per cent for some commodities and 12.5 per cent for others, and was now raised to a general rate of 15 per cent.

Another important taxation change was less controversial in character. The Petroleum Revenue Tax (PRT) had been introduced by the outgoing Labour Government, at the rate of 45 per cent. Before that administration left office, plans existed to increase the figure to 60 per cent, and these were put into effect in the first Conservative budget. This change coincided with an enormous increase in the volumes of oil and gas extracted from the new North Sea fields. In 1978–9, the yield of the PRT had been £183 million; in the following year it was £1,435 million, after which it continued to rise steeply. A supplementary petroleum duty was added in 1981 and the yield of the two taxes peaked at over £7,000 million in 1984–5. By that date it amounted to more than 8 per cent of the total tax revenue of Central government.

Howe was Chancellor for four years, but his subsequent budgets were far less radical in character than the first one had been. The general effect of the Government's policy however, was to produce a substantial shift in the burden of taxation. In the tax year 1978–9, the combined yield of Income Tax, the vestiges of Surtax, and Corporation Tax, had been 55.6 per cent of the total government tax revenue, while customs and excise produced 3.7 per cent. In the tax year 1982–83, the corresponding figures were 47.2 per cent and 36.6 per cent.[2]

The General Election of 1983 confirmed the Conservatives in office, but Howe moved from the Exchequer to the Foreign Office, and was succeeded by Nigel Lawson, a man of a more original mind, disposed to take risks. In 1984, Lawson decided to phase out tax reliefs for business, but also to cut Corporation Tax and to abolish the remaining National Insurance surcharge.

Lawson remained at the Exchequer from 1983 until his spectacular resignation in 1989. In that period, other substantial changes in taxation were recorded. The ordinary taxpayer noted progressive cuts in Income Tax. By 1988, the basic rate was stabilised at 25 per cent, the top rate at 40 per cent. It is remarkable, however, that the proportional yield of Income Tax and Corporation Tax together had increased, making 51.1 per cent of the total. [3]

Other important taxation changes were made during the period of Lawson's Chancellorship. The Development Land Tax had been introduced in 1974 in order to collect increases in land values deriving from inflation and speculation. It did not prove very effective in that regard, but it had discouraged people from developing land. The tax was abolished in 1985. It was soon perceived that the Capital Transfer Tax, which had also been introduced in 1974, had not collected much revenue from gifts *inter vivos*, and it was replaced by a simple Inheritance Tax.

In the 1980s, the central government's policy towards local government, and in particular towards local government spending and taxation, came to exert a profound effect on the whole political scene. A radical change of some kind was long overdue. Originally, local authorities had raised money mainly for strictly local purposes like the relief of poverty and for public works. As time went on, those functions were largely taken over by central government, while at the same time local authorities were given new and very expensive duties, notably in connexion with education and social services. These required large subventions from central government and a very complicated system of Rate Support Grants was developed. In the 1980s, local authority spending represented about a quarter of all public expenditure, while something like half of this money was provided by the Treasury,[4] the remainder being drawn overwhelmingly from rates.

The local authorities had wide discretion over spending, and there was much press and public criticism of the way in which some of them exercised that discretion. The Government was disposed to think that the profligacy of some local authorities had been much encouraged by the fact that many local government electors were not ratepayers and so had little to lose from such policies. In the first half of the 1980s measures designed to control local government spending were introduced. Most famous of these was 'rate capping', by which the spending powers of local authorities were drastically limited.

In March 1985, the Prime Minister and some of her colleagues discussed a new system, or rather two parallel systems, of local government finance. Rating, it was suggested, should be abolished for domestic property and should be replaced by a new 'community charge'. This soon became generally known as the 'Poll Tax', to the chagrin of the Prime Minister. Businesses would pay a Uniform Business Rate (UBR). The UBR, as the name suggested, would be uniform throughout the country, and would not be related to the financial needs of the particular authority in which the business was situated. The Poll Tax would be charged at the same level for all adults within the local authority concerned, save for relief in cases of special need. Thus the value of the property in which the local taxpayer resided would normally be irrelevant. In the view of the Prime Minister, 'everyone should contribute something and therefore have something to lose from electing a spendthrift council'.[5] Not all ministers were happy about the Poll Tax proposals. The Chancellor of the Exchequer expressed particularly serious doubts,[6] and a long period of discussions took place. At one point, special attention was given to what became known as 'dual running', which would involve a long transition period from the old system of local taxation to the new; but that idea was later abandoned.

A curious accident gave local taxation reform some urgency. As the law stood, there was no requirement that rating valuations in England and Wales should be held at particular intervals – the last one had been in 1973 – but here was a statutory obligation to revalue rateable property in Scotland at five-year intervals. It would been absurd to incur the expense and possible political obloquy which a revaluation would involve and then soon afterwards scrap it in favour of a different system. The Government therefore introduced its proposals for the new system in Scotland, though not for England and Wales. These became law shortly before the General Election of 1987, but did not take immediate effect.

Discussions about the Community Charge did not play much part in the election except in Scotland, where its effect seems to have been politically 'neutral'.[7] But when steps were taken towards implementation, the controversy became intense. It was first applied in Scotland in 1989, amid massive and noisy opposition. Meanwhile, parallel legislation for England and Wales was prepared. This ran into considerable difficulties in Parliament and there were substantial revolts of Conservative MPs, but it eventually became law early in 1990.

There followed large demonstrations, some of a violent nature. A great many people who were required by law to register for Poll Tax failed to do so, and there were widespread instances of non-payment, in some cases reaching 50 per cent of those liable.[8] A year later , it was officially admitted that some £2000 million, or 10 per cent of the budgeted sum, was uncollected. Nigel Lawson later wrote dramatically of the response in his own constituency:

> What was unsupportable was the anguish caused to millions of ordinary people ... In all my years as an M.P. I have never encountered anything like it. Constituents of modest means would come to me, asking me why they should suddenly be faced with this huge increase in their local tax bills, and there was no convincing answer I could possibly give them.[9]

Various expedients were devised to cope with the crisis. Local councils were forced to take out loans to meet the shortfall. In July 1990, it was announced that transitional relief would be extended to no fewer than 11.5 million people, and that the Treasury would contribute an extra £3,260 million to local government for 1991–2.

All this, of course, was completely outside the intention, or even the contemplation, of these who had promoted the idea of the Poll Tax, and there can be little doubt in retrospect that the immense public controversy on the matter was of critical importance – more important, perhaps, than any other single factor – in driving Margaret Thatcher from the premiership in November 1990.

Meanwhile, other important changes had begun to take effect. In October 1989, Nigel Lawson resigned from the post of Chancellor of the Exchequer on an issue apparently unrelated to the Poll Tax. His successor, John Major, was author of the 1990 budget. This was a relatively mild affair, whose most famous feature was the introduction of TESSAs – authorising a new form of investment carrying tax relief. More significantly, perhaps, Major was compelled to announce that the large reduction in the Public Sector Debt Repayment which had been forecast by his predecessor would be halved.

Major had, however, advanced to a very important place in the Government. When the Conservative leadership, and therefore the premiership, was contested a year later, he eventually emerged, rather unexpectedly, as the victor.

The new Ministry was bound to take early action to limit the damage which flowed from the Poll Tax. In his budget speech of March 1991, Norman Lamont, the new Chancellor, proposed a cut of £140 per head in Poll Tax, which would be accompanied by an increase in VAT from

15 per cent to 17.5 per cent. He also revealed a dramatic change in the source of local government finance which had been caused by the episode. In 1991–2, only 22 per cent of the money would be raised from local sources.

When the Major Government was formed, Michael Heseltine, a declared opponent of the Poll Tax, was appointed Secretary of State for the Environment – that is, the Minister responsible for local government. The new system of local government taxation which parliament approved in 1991 and which took effect in the following year had every appearance of an uneasy compromise. The UBR was retained for business premises, but in place of the Community Charge what was called a Council Tax would be levied on domestic property. This had some resemblance to the old rating system, but the property was to be set in seven – later eight – broad bands, related to the apparent market value at the height of the recent property boom. Another feature of the new arrangement was that the owner of property with a single adult occupant would only pay 75 per cent as much as when there were two or more occupants. This was represented as a concession to single occupants, but it could be regarded equally well as a poll tax on the second occupant.

Many observers anticipated that the fall of Margaret Thatcher in November 1990, and repudiation of the policy which she had taken so much to her heart, less than six months later, would be followed by her party's defeat at the ensuing General Election. That event seemed the more likely as there were increasing signs of economic depression as the date of that election approached. But Major's Government secured a renewed lease of life, though with a much reduced majority, at the General Election of April 1992.

Central government taxation policy in the post-Thatcher era showed both similarities and differences from that of the 1980s. If Lamont's first budget had been concerned essentially with damage limitation, his second budget, introduced just before the 1992 General Election, seemed to mark a further development of the established Conservative policy of steadily reducing direct taxation. In the 1980s, this policy had been conducted mainly by progressive reductions in the basic rate of Income Tax and the rate of Corporation Tax. The 1992 budget established what might perhaps be called two basic rates of Income Tax: a rate of 20 per cent on the first £2,000 of taxable income, while the old basic rate of 25 per cent remained above that level. This policy was extended in Lamont's 1993 budget, for the bottom level of taxable income at which the lower rate operated was raised to £2,500 for 1993–4, with the promise of £3,000 for the following year. There would also be substantial reductions in Corporation Tax.

Such a policy implied further taxation elsewhere, and the most controversial measure proposed in 1993 was an extension of VAT to domestic fuel and power, at a rate of 8 per cent for 1994–5, rising to the general VAT rate of 17.5 per cent in 1995–6. Critics contended that the new tax would bear most heavily on poor people and particularly on elderly people, who in many cases would be driven to reduce domestic heating, sometimes at risk of their very lives.

This controversy was gathering momentum when Lamont resigned office on a different issue, in June 1993. He was replaced as Chancellor by Kenneth Clarke. A change which had been foreshadowed some years earlier came into effect at the beginning of Clarke's period in office. The old division between an expenditure statement in the late autumn and a taxation budget in the spring was broken, and Clarke's first 'all-purpose' budget was introduced in November 1993. The new Chancellor made important changes in Social Security benefits and a number of relatively small tax increases, notably on road fuel and tobacco. This budget also saw the introduction of a new airport departures tax.

The debate on domestic fuel VAT was resumed in the course of discussions about Clarke's second budget, of November 1994. The initial establishment of the tax at 8 per cent had taken effect in April 1994, but the further rise to the general VAT level of 17.5 per cent was checked. A critical motion from Opposition benches was supported by a small, but sufficient, number of Conservative MPs. The Government's overall majority in the House of Commons was small, and this revolt was enough to upset it. The Chancellor thereupon announced that the increase would not occur, but instead that other tax increases, notably on alcohol, tobacco and road fuel, would take its place.

One may suspect that this turn of events was not wholly displeasing to some members of the Government. The developing controversy had some features in common with what had happened in the early days of the Poll Tax debate; and the prospect of another protracted and politically damaging dispute over a matter of taxation which was in no sense vital either to national finances or the general policy of the government, must have set many alarm bells ringing.

On the assumption that the Government would delay a General Election to almost the latest date which was legally possible, two further annual budgets were required. Clarke presided over both of those budgets. Each continued the essential Conservative taxation policies of reducing public expenditure relative to the Gross Domestic Product, and in particular of reducing direct taxation. So far as Income Tax was concerned, the old approach of reducing the main basic rate was followed, rather than the

Lamont approach of raising the level at which the lowest rate applied. In November 1995, the main basic rate was brought down from 25 per cent to 24 per cent, and in November 1996 it was further reduced to 23 per cent for the financial year 1997–8. This policy, however, required increased taxes on such items as tobacco, road fuel and airport travel.

Thus stood the level of taxation on the eve of the General Election of May 1997, which was to result in defeat for the Conservatives and establishment of a Labour Government with a very comfortable majority. Great changes had certainly taken place since the Conservatives assumed office in 1979. The ordinary taxpayer no doubt noticed most keenly the decline of Income Tax, whose basic rate had stood at 33 per cent when the Conservatives took office, but had been reduced to 23 per cent when they left 18 years later. By contrast, however, VAT, which had stood at 8 per cent for some items and 12.5 per cent for others in early 1979, was currently 17.5 per cent for most things. Some items were still altogether exempt, while domestic fuel – thanks to the revolt of 1994 – was taxed at only 8 per cent.

These changes were part of wider developments in the pattern of taxation. Yet it is easy to exaggerate some of the differences in actual results, as opposed to Ministerial intentions. In 1978–9, the revenue of central government was £65,242 million, or 39.7 per cent of a Gross Domestic Product of £164,165 million based on current prices.[10] In 1995–6, revenue was £270,200 million, or 36.7 per cent of a GDP of £735,575 million.

The relative yields of different kinds of taxes underwent changes too. The big increase was VAT, which in 1978–9 produced 7.4 per cent of central government income and in 1995–6 produced 15.9 per cent. The yield of taxes on income – excluding Corporation Tax – decreased considerably, but less dramatically than might have been anticipated in view of the sustained policy of Income Tax rate reduction. In 1978–9 they produced 38.4 per cent of central government income; in 1995–6 they produced 34.4 per cent.[11]

15 Overview

In 1660, £1.2 million of public money was promised for the needs of Charles II. Budgets of the late 1990s contemplate taxation receipts far in excess of £200,000 million. When the widest possible allowances are made for population growth, for the larger size of the realm and for inflation, the taxation burden per head has increased by a factor of far more than 100. The change has not been regular throughout the period; there have been long periods of relative stability, interspersed with periods of frenetic taxation growth. Just as there have been vast changes in the total amount of taxation, so also have there been great changes in the purposes for which taxes have been collected, and the items which have been taxed.

At the time of the Restoration, just as today, taxes were levied to pay for items which most people agreed were necessary, but which, by the nature of things, the citizen could not – or would not – discharge for himself. A merchant could not adequately protect his own ships from attack and required help from the King's ships to achieve that protection. Parishioners were unlikely to provide adequate money for relief of poverty or for the construction of roads and bridges through acts of private and voluntary charity, and so a system of local rating was required.

In the mid-seventeenth century, however, most taxes (though customs duties were an important exception here) were not perceived as burdens which the citizen must go on bearing for the whole foreseeable future, but rather as devices which were called into being from time to time to meet some special need. Rates were levied as and when there were paupers to support, or public works to be undertaken. 'Aids', poll taxes and hearth taxes were demanded as and when required.

The idea that taxes should be linked with specific items of expenditure has persisted into the twentieth century. When taxes on motor fuel and cars were introduced in 1909, those taxes were initially earmarked for purposes of road construction and maintenance, although this link was soon broken. National Insurance contributions (which many people perceive as taxes in all but name) are still linked to the insured person's right to benefits. Most contemporary taxes, however, have no link with any specific item of expenditure. Taxes are paid into a common pool, from which public spending is drawn as required.

Just as all government is by consent of the governed, so is all taxation by consent of the taxpayer. This rule applies both to the total volume of tax collected, and to the individual items on which it is charged. But changes of attitude towards the amount of taxation which is tolerable, as well as attitudes towards individual taxes, have often taken place with considerable speed.

Wars are of particular importance in this respect, for they accustom taxpayers to much higher levels of taxation than they experienced before, and the changed attitudes persist to a large extent in the ensuing peace. At the accession of William III, central government revenue was below £3 million a year. After the almost continuous wars of William and his successor Anne, it exceeded £5.5 million, and never again fell substantially below that level. At the outbreak of the Seven Years War in 1756, revenue stood at a shade over £7 million; when the war came to an end it exceeded £10 million. Just before the French revolutionary and Napoleonic Wars began, central government revenue was a little below £19 million; by 1816 it had reached over £79 million. Even the best efforts of nineteenth-century governments determined to practise economy never brought it below £50 million. In 1914, national taxation was still below £190 million; by 1919 it stood at £889 million, and was never again brought perceptibly below £800 million. In 1938, the figure was just under £950 million; by 1946 it was £3,400 million, and has never been brought below that figure.

The reasons why major wars are invariably accompanied by quantum leaps in taxation which continue after the war in over are not difficult to understand. One important factor is the increase in taxation required to pay interest on the increased National Debt occasioned by the war. In most cases, it is doubtful whether a government which was conducting a war would have been able to maintain public support for so doing if the taxpayers had been required to pay immediately the full cost of a warlike policy. So a large part of that cost has been shifted on to posterity, and it remains necessary to service the National Debt.

There is another more subtle reason why wars are regularly associated with increases in taxation. Taxpayers who became accustomed to paying more money in order to defray some of the perceived needs of wartime soon almost forgot the relatively low taxation they enjoyed before fighting commenced.

Since the 1939–45 war, a new factor has affected taxpayers' control over government spending and consequential taxation. Inflation, which at most times in our history has been slow, has become much more rapid in the second half of the twentieth century. True, the two-figure inflation which marked part of the 1970s and 1980s appears to be a thing of the past; but an annual inflation rate of around 3 per cent, which in most periods would have been considered appallingly high, is today regarded as a creditable performance. The public is so familiar with increases in all prices of goods and services that it has tacitly accepted taxation increases as well. Again, the old standards of reference have been largely lost.

At times, however, the taxpayer worm will turn. There have been various examples in the present story in which the government of the day sought to impose or to retain particular taxes, but these were eventually abandoned because numerous quite ordinary people decided that they did not like them. The seventeenth-century Poll Tax and Hearth Tax were quietly dropped because they were unpopular. The equally unpopular late twentieth-century Community Charge was also dropped.

What makes people willing to pay one tax but unwilling to pay another is not just a simple matter of how much it costs. In 1733, there was huge, and effective, resistance to 'general excise', yet landed gentlemen continued to pay the 'Land Tax' without much protest. Partly, one might say, this attitude was linked with the apparently temporary character of the 'Land Tax' and the more permanent character of 'general excise'; but there was also the very important, and perhaps overriding, consideration that landowners preferred to pay taxes which had been fixed by other landowners, rather than taxes assessed by obscure public officials.

Attitudes towards particular taxes change considerably over time. In 1799, Pitt encountered considerable opposition to his Income Tax proposals, which were resented not only as new burdens on the taxpayer, but also because they were considered inquisitorial. He was only able to carry his proposals because nobody could think of any other way of raising the money necessary to beat the forces of revolutionary France. As soon as the opportunity presented itself, Income Tax was swept away, to the high embarrassment of the Government. Yet between 1816 and 1842 public attitudes underwent a huge change and Peel was able to restore Income Tax because it was generally seen as preferable to a mass of indirect taxes.

Patterns of taxation which were brought into existence to meet one set of circumstances persist long after those circumstances have changed. Wartime taxation is the prime example, but it is not the only example. The reason seems to be that familiarity with a tax, or with a pattern of taxation, breeds toleration rather than contempt. Once the new arrangement has been in existence for a number of years, it tends to 'fossilise'.

The eighteenth-century 'Land Tax' provides a good example. Originally, it was not designed as specifically a land tax at all, but rather as a general tax on wealth. It gradually came to fall overwhelmingly on what lawyers call 'land', because of the difficulty of assessing other kinds of assets, and stuck as a 'Land Tax', in that sense of the word 'land', for the remainder of its existence.

The 'Land Tax' 'fossilised' in other ways as well. The basis on which personal assessments were made, as well as the assessments of specific counties or towns, soon became fixed at the levels at which they had stood in 1692, because the periodic revisions which were necessary to keep them up to date were sure to occasion storms of protest from those about to be disadvantaged, and it is common experience that the protests of likely losers are much more noisy than the approbation of likely gainers. The tax had originally been collected at a variable rate and at variable intervals. By the late eighteenth-century, however, it was so firmly fixed at the annual rate of 20 per cent on the 1692 valuation that Pitt was able to offer to commute the tax for a cash payment on that basis. More astonishing still, Pitt's commutation figure, and the 'Land Tax' which had to be paid by those who did not choose to commute, still remained in force for a century and a half after his death. In the second half of the twentieth century, this money was still being paid on the basis of a valuation more than 250 years old, which had not been very accurate when it was first drawn up.

Modern taxes exhibit the same tendency to 'fossilise'. When VAT began in the early 1970s, it was fixed at 10 per cent. This figure at least had the merit of being easy to calculate. For several years thereafter, VAT varied according to perceived revenue needs and variations in general economic policy. For a time there were different rates applicable to different goods and services.

In 1979, there was a deliberate shift from direct towards indirect taxation, and this resulted in a general increase in VAT to a single rate of 15 per cent, at which level it remained until 1991. Then an emergency arose. The government found it necessary to reduce the Community Charge, payable to local authorities. To compensate for this reduction and the consequential loss of revenue, VAT was increased to 17.5 per cent. Not long afterwards, the Community Charge was abolished altogether, and replaced by a different system of local taxation. Yet VAT remained, and still remains at the time of writing in the beginning of 1999, at 17.5 per cent, having survived a change of government in 1997. That figure is most inconvenient for calculations, but it is a sum which people have been accustomed to paying, and for that reason it has been preserved.

Once a tax is firmly established, its social and economic effects may gradually change, but new arguments are usually presented for keeping it. As has been noted several times, customs duties were originally imposed to levy revenue to help the King protect shipping against enemies. When the risk of attack abated, they gradually became a useful source of revenue for other purposes. Then, in the middle years of the nineteenth century, many economic assumptions were suddenly called into question, including the usefulness of customs duties. On a few occasions, notably in 1842 and in 1860, some reforming Minister made a bonfire of dozens or even hundreds of these taxes, with negligible loss of revenue.

In the closing years of the nineteenth century and the early twentieth century, there was a swing the other way. Customs duties came into favour again in certain quarters, though for two very different reasons. Some people perceived that direct taxation posed a serious threat to the wealthier classes, and spoke of 'broadening the basis of taxation'. Other people, who were fearful of the effects which foreign competition might have on their livelihoods, moved to Protectionism under the new name 'Tariff Reform'.

However, the major change in fortune for customs duties did not come for either of these reasons, for in the 1914 war a spate of new customs duties was applied in order to discourage imports of luxury goods and thereby to save shipping space. These taxes, the 'McKenna Duties', were continued after the war, save for a brief interruption in 1924, and gradually acquired 'respectability'. Then, in 1932, an acute economic crisis arose, and many people were persuaded to accept a large extension to customs duties. Just like the Free Trade 'breakthrough', which was achieved through repeal of the Corn Laws in 1846, the Protectionist 'breakthrough' of 1932 had little to do with any change in the respective arguments for Free Trade and Protection. In both cases, major economic crises disposed people to accept new policies.

The history of Income Tax since 1842 is another striking example of the way in which a tax may gradually change in character. Early Income Tax was a 'minority tax', with the great majority of citizens well beyond its reach. Thus, the 1871 census disclosed a UK population of just under 31.5 million, while only 468,000, or fewer than 1.5 per cent of the whole, paid Schedule D income tax.[1] In 1873–4, the yield of Income Tax was only £5.6 million, and the tax level was down to 2d in the pound, or less than 1 per cent. At the time of the 1874 General Election, when Gladstone advocated complete removal of Income Tax, this was quite a realistic suggestion. Income Tax was saved by increasing demands on the public exchequer, and by the early twentieth century few voices called for its removal in the near future. In the next few years, it proved very useful in helping to finance social legislation and rearmament, and when war came in 1914 the level of Income Tax was rapidly increased. In the 1939 war, the level rose again, the standard rate eventually reaching 50 per cent of income. By this stage, it had attained, or perhaps exceeded, the most productive level, and since then there has been a gradual, but intermittent, decline in levels, while the number of taxpayers has increased so much that it has become perhaps the most 'universal' tax of all.

Corresponding changes of pattern may be traced in other taxes as well; but an even more striking development has been the change in functions which taxation is meant to discharge. Provision of the enormous sums required to finance public health, the social services, communications and education is an obvious example.

An important development in taxation from the late nineteenth century onwards has derived from the idea that it ought to exert an important function in redistributing wealth – something much more extensive than the relief of dire poverty. It derives from the conviction, not always stated expressly, that the rich are a good deal richer, and the poor are a good deal poorer, than ought to be the case.

Examples of legislation designed, at least in part, to produce more social equality go back more than a century. Harcourt's 1894 budget graded death duties steeply. The underlying idea seems to have been, at least in part, the view that great accumulations of wealth made by one generation should not be passed on, in their entirety, to future generations. Lloyd George's 1909 budget advanced the idea of redistribution through taxation further. This time the current generation was targeted as well as future generations, and a Super Tax on high incomes was introduced. As the twentieth century advanced, it became generally accepted that wealthy people should contribute a good deal more in taxation than they could expect to recoup in direct benefits.

Another important feature of modern taxation is the disposition of governments to tax items with the object of changing patterns of consumption. 'Protectionist' policies in peacetime were designed to restrict consumption of foreign goods in general, for the presumed benefit of domestic, or imperial, producers. There is a much older practice of discouraging the consumption of particular kinds of goods because they are considered harmful to the consumer, or to other people. Duties on alcoholic drinks provide a good example. The earliest taxation on drinks, whether through customs or excise, was designed purely for revenue purposes. Yet taxes were imposed on gin in the first half of the eighteenth century, not primarily for revenue, but to discourage heavy drinking. In the second part of the nineteenth century, and in the twentieth century, taxes on alcoholic drinks of all kinds were widely applied for similar reasons.

Tobacco taxes have followed a comparable pattern. For a long time, they were merely a source of revenue; but from the 1950s onwards there has been a growing realisation that tobacco is responsible for an enormous amount of illness and premature death, and so tobacco taxation has acquired an important function in discouraging consumption. Governments, however, have often taken an ambivalent attitude to the problem. They have not always been disposed to incur substantial revenue losses by taxing tobacco at a rate which would have a serious effect on sales.

More recently still, sales of petrol and other road fuels have begun to pose similar problems for the taxgatherer. When road fuel taxes were first proposed in 1909, petrol-using vehicles were almost exclusively a luxury of rich men. Within a very short time, motor buses and motor taxis appeared on the roads, and eventually the car itself became a vehicle of general use. Taxes on vehicles and road fuel became increasingly important. For many years, the Treasury was happy that the new goose should continue laying golden eggs, and did not choose to risk impairing the bird's productivity. Recently, however, there has been growing concern about the environmental effects of pollution deriving from use of motor fuels. The Government has found itself in the rather unusual position of facing a widespread public demand for increases in taxation and has been induced to raise fuel taxes in order to discourage car use. It has also taxed fuels selectively, imposing heavier taxes on fuels considered to be particularly harmful to the environment than on others.

An important feature of taxation which has not always attracted enough attention when a new tax was initially proposed is the very complex effects which taxes often produce, which are sometimes completely at variance with the original intentions of the legislature. This has been particularly important in the twentieth century, when taxes have often been designed to do much more than raise revenue; indeed, the revenue-raising function is sometimes of small importance.

A good example is the Development Charge which accompanied the Town and Country Planning Act of 1947. The tax was originally designed to ensure that when land appreciated in value because it was required for development, the increased value of that land which accrued to the owner should be collected for the public exchequer. The object of the Development Charge was clearly to discourage land speculation rather than to raise revenue.

Parliament provided that the Development Charge should be paid, not when the land appreciated in value, but when it was actually developed. As a result, the Development Charge became a powerful disincentive for development. Landowners who guessed (rightly, as it proved) that a new government would repeal the Development Charge kept their land undeveloped while its market value was increasing, and eventually sold it at a great profit when the Development Charge was abolished. Thus a tax which had been designed to discourage speculation in rising land values and to encourage development where this was authorised by planning law produced exactly the opposite result.

A significant modern change in taxation policy has been the special arrangements made for corporations. They had long been subject to Income Tax, and in both world wars special taxes, which in practice fell largely on corporations, were introduced with the object of collecting excess profits deriving from wartime activities. In the case of both wars, the special taxes were repealed shortly after the conflict ended. In 1946, however, with the ending of the Excess Profits Tax, the wartime National Defence Contribution was renamed the Profits Tax, and for the next 20 years corporations were liable for both Income Tax and Profits Tax.

A new Corporation Tax to replace those two taxes was foreshadowed late in 1964, and took effect in 1966. It was to be levied at a flat rate on the total income of the corporation. Deductions would be made for normal interest (including interest on debentures) and on other charges, but not for interest on ordinary or preference shares, where the recipients would be liable for Income Tax and (while it lasted) Surtax. This arrangement appears to have had some effect in disposing corporations to take out loans rather than to issue equity capital.

The unintended results of modern taxation often derive from the fact that it is produced in a hurry, to meet some emergency, and not as part of a considered policy. The proposal to introduce a Community Charge was debated for several years at a high level of government; but there were no definite conclusions. When the need to apply a new system of local taxation to Scotland galvanised the government into action, there is little reason for thinking that anybody had studied closely the full economic consequences, still less the social and political consequences, which were likely to follow, whether in Scotland or elsewhere.

When the Community Charge proved intensely unpopular, and was also very difficult to collect, a new Council Tax eventually emerged to replace it. There were fewer positive arguments in favour of the Council Tax than either the old rating system or the Community Charge. It was a good deal less precise than rating, and the principle that everyone should have a stake in the efficiency of local government which had inspired the Community Charge was absent. The Council Tax had every appearance of being an uneasy compromise, designed to avoid giving too much offence to anybody in the Government, and to avoid causing too much trouble with the general public.

These may appear to be extreme examples of taxes producing results completely different from those originally contemplated; but nearly all taxes generate some more or less unanticipated side-effects. Customs duties or excise duties have had a substantial effect on labour and capital, deflecting them from one activity to another. If the importation of some commodities is discouraged by customs duties, it is probably intended that there should be a movement of labour and capital into home production of the goods on which the duties fall. But it is only possible to pay for imports by exports, and so goods or services which would otherwise have been produced for the export market will not be provided. As a result, there will be wide changes in patterns of employment and investment in export industries.

A modern tax like VAT also has a complex effect. VAT falls partly on goods, where the tax discourages people from adding value by applying new processes to those goods. It also falls partly on services, where it discourages people from providing those services. A person who discovers that the bill for decorating his house or servicing his car will be increased by 17.5 per cent to cover VAT will often leave his house undecorated or his car unserviced; or he may attempt the job himself. VAT is therefore bound to have a very substantial effect on the use of both capital and labour, and on levels of unemployment.

To a large extent, the unanticipated side-effects of taxes derive from the fact that a particular tax usually falls on several different kinds of economic activity. Income Tax must be paid whether the income derives from work, from investment in industry or from speculation on land prices. Similarly, VAT falls on luxuries and on necessities, on goods and on services.

In order to examine more closely the way in which taxes have operated, it is useful to note the division between factors of production which was drawn by the classical economists of the late eighteenth and nineteenth centuries. As has been noted before, 'Land' meant all natural resources. The site on which a house or a factory rests is 'land'; the building itself is not. 'Labour' meant all human effort, physical or mental. 'Capital' meant things which were made available for human use by the action of labour upon land. A spade or a machine, or goods on a shopkeeper's shelf, were 'capital' in that sense of the word. 'Capital' was not equated with money. Indeed, money is not a factor of production at all, but a medium of exchange, which may be used to purchase land, or labour, or capital.

From the standpoint of taxation, there is a vital difference between land on one side, and labour and capital on the other. Quantities of labour and capital are not fixed, and each can usually be moved from one place or activity to another. The quantity and the location of land cannot be changed. Familiar taxes usually fall on two or more of the three factors of production, and they have very different effects.

To make matters appear even more confusing, the very names of taxes sometimes mislead people as to what their targets were. The eighteenth century 'Land Tax' applied not only to land (in the economist's sense of the word), but also be capital. The twentieth century Capital Transfer Tax applied not only to transfer of capital but also to transfer of land. The Capital Gains Tax applied to gains in the value of capital, but also to gains in the value of land.

By contrast with taxes on labour and capital, with their many unintended and unforeseen consequences, a tax which falls on land alone is remarkably direct and simple in its effects. It can have no effect on supply, for the quantity of land in existence is unalterable. A tax on land will, however, affect the availability of land, but its effect will be completely different in that respect from the effect of a tax on labour or capital.

Much land is kept out of use, or is not used in the most suitable way permitted by planning law, because it suits the owner to withhold it for speculative or other reasons. The value of a piece of land is related to the use to which the land *can* be put, not to the use to which it currently *is* put. So a tax on the value of land is also not affected by the use to which that land is actually put. If the value of land is taxed, the owner is encouraged to use the land in the most productive way which planning law permits, or to dispose of it to someone who will do so. Thus the effect of a tax on land would be to increase that amount of land available for use, while the usual effect of a tax on labour or capital is the opposite. A mixed tax, which falls partly on land and partly on capital or labour, would be bound to have mixed consequences.

One general problem of taxation has become particularly acute in the late twentieth century. How far is the taxpayer receiving value for money? It is possible to discover how much it costs the government to collect a tax, but it is much more difficult to discover how much it really cost the citizen to pay that tax. How does one cost the labour of a person filling up forms for Income Tax or VAT? What expenses must a firm incur when it needs to employ people to draw up and supply the information demanded by governments, or to avoid paying tax for which it is not lawfully liable?

Another 'value for money' problem of a different kind arises. In the nineteenth century, it was possible for an energetic and meticulous statesman like Gladstone to keep a detailed watch on all public spending. Today, that would be out of the question. Expenditure takes place on a scale which goes beyond the comprehension of most citizens, and taxation must match it.

People have come to feel increasingly helpless and confused about the impact of taxation on their daily lives. The average annual taxation demands of central government alone are in excess of £5,000 for every man, woman and child in the country. Since 1914, the levy of taxation has multiplied more than a 1000 fold. Money values have changed greatly, but not as much as that. Many people consider that a great deal of the money levied in taxation is spent unwisely, and that the manner in which taxes are collected is also often unwise, but that there seems little they can do – or even that governments can do – to control processes which have acquired their own momentum.

Yet the historian recalls occasions on which apparently helpless and powerless people have contrived to alter taxation patterns substantially. Various examples have been considered: abolition of the seventeenth century Hearth Tax and Poll Tax; the defeat of 'general excise' in the eighteenth century; abolition of Income Tax in 1816, and of the Corn Laws in 1846. Much more recently, the excitement generated around 1990 by the Community Charge bore little relation to the amount of money which was likely to be collected thereby; what people did note was that the new tax seemed a grossly unfair innovation. Examples where there was popular pressure for new taxation are less frequent, but in the early twentieth century there was immense public enthusiasm for the taxation of land values, and there is every reason for thinking that this demand would have taken effect if war had not intervened and changed everything beyond recognition.

Thus a widespread belief that a tax is just, or that it is unjust, really does have an effect on whether or not it takes root. It would be unhistoric to regard issues of taxation as no more than a power struggle between interest groups, or between statesmen avid to make political points against each other. Real issues of principle continue to arise, even in matters of taxation. Taxpayers may change their minds from time to time as to how much money may properly be collected in taxation, or which particular taxes are unfair in principle or too severe in their incidence. But the statesman who flies in the teeth of the taxpayers' current judgement does so at his peril. Charles I, George Grenville, Nicholas Vansittart and Margaret Thatcher are examples from different centuries of people who have failed – to their cost – to take that important lesson.

Notes

CHAPTER 1

1. See discussion in William Kennedy, *English Taxation 1640–1799* (London 1913).
2. B.E.V. Sabine, *A Short History of Taxation* (London 1980), p. 93.
3. J.P. Kenyon, *Stuart England* (Harmondsworth 1978).
4. Sabine, *op. cit.*
5. David Ogg, *England in the Reign of Charles II* (Oxford 1956), p. 439.
6. The various arguments are well discussed in Kennedy, *op. cit.*
7. Sabine, *op. cit.*
8. See Henry Roseveare, *The Treasury 1660–1870* (London 1973); George Clark, *The Later Stuarts 1660–1714* (Oxford 1985).
9. Stephen B. Baxter, *The Development of the Treasury 1660–1702* (London 1957), p. 86.
10. See Christopher Hill, *The Century of Revolution 1603–1714* (Walton-on-Thames 1980).
11. Edward Hughes, *Studies in Administraton and Finance 1558–1825* (Manchester 1934).
12. John Brewer, *The Sinews of Power ... 1688–1783* (London 1989).
13. Until 1752, the year began on 25 March. Events which took place from 1 January to 24 March, which contemporaries attributed to one year and most modern writers attribute to the ensuing year, are here set in this form.
14. Baxter, *op. cit.*; see also Roseveare, *op. cit.*
15. Roseveare, *op. cit.*, p. 23.
16. Hill, *op. cit.*, pp. 186–7.

CHAPTER 2

1. See Edward Hughes, *Studies in Administration and Finance 1558–1825* (Manchester 1934); Henry Roseveare, *The Financial Revolution 1660–1760* (London and N.Y. 1991).
2. Roseveare, *op. cit.*, p. 307.
3. Stephen Dowell, *A History of Taxation and Taxes in England* (first edn. 1884; third edn. 1965) vol. 2, p. 43.
4. Dowell, *op. cit.*, vol. 2, p. 44.
5. For a detailed discussion, see J.V. Beckett, 'Land Tax or Excise: the Levying of Taxation in Seventeenth- and Eighteenth-century England', *Eng. Hist. Rev.* (1985), pp. 285–308. See also B.E.V. Sabine, *A Short History of Taxation* (London 1980).
6. Gul. et Mar. 1 cap. 20.
7. See David Ogg, *England in the Reigns of James II and William III* (Oxford 1984).

8.   Dowell, *op. cit.*, vol. 2, p. 50.
9.   Ogg, *op. cit.*
10. Ibid., p. 414.
11. John Brewer, *The Sinews of Power... 1688–1783* (London 1989), p. 40.
12. Ibid., p. 30.
13. Figures calculated from D.W. Jones, *War and Economy in the Age of William III and Marlborough* (Oxford 1988) p. 70.
14. See P. and F. Somerset Fry, *The History of Scotland* (London 1982), pp. 182–90.

CHAPTER 3

1.   Figures of the National Debt and of the interest thereon, and other statistics used in this chapter, are based on B.R. Mitchell, *British Historical Statistics* (Cambridge 1988), and the sources there used.
2.   Brian W. Hill, *Sir Robert Walpole* (London, 1989), p. 171.
3.   Stephen Dowell, *A History of Taxation and Taxes in England* (first edn. 1884; third edn. 1965) vol. 2, p. 96.
4.   See, in particular, the discussion in William Kennedy, *English Taxation 1640–1799* (London 1913), p. 99 *et seq.*
5.   See J.V. Beckett, 'Land Tax or Excise ...', *Eng. Hist. Rev.* (April 1985) pp. 285–308.
6.   I.S. Leadam, *The Political History of England... 1702–1760* (London 1909; N.Y. reprint, 1969), pp. 350–1.
7.   Dowell, *op. cit.*, p. 118.
8.   See discussion in Henry Roseveare, *The Financial Revolution 1660–1760* (London and N.Y., 1991), p. 62.
9.   John Brewer, *The Sinews of Power ...* (London 1990), p. 40.
10. Robert A. Becker, *Revolution, Reform and the Politics of American Taxation 1763–1783* (Louisiana State University Press 1980), p. 6.
11. See James Coffield: *A Popular History of Taxation* (London 1970), pp. 82–3.
12. Ibid., p. 84.

CHAPTER 4

1.   Edwin R. Seligman, *The Income Tax* (N.Y., 1911), p. 62.
2.   Étienne Martin, *Les impôts directs en Angleterre ...* (Paris &c., 1905), pp. 208–9.
3.   See discussion in R.B. McDowell article in T.W. Moody and W.E. Vaughan, eds., *A New History of Ireland* (Oxford 1986) vol. iv.
4.   G.C. Brodrick and J.K. Fotheringham, *History of England... 801–1837* (London &c 1909; N.Y. reprint 1969), p. 15.
5.   Figures based on Stephen Dowell, *A History of Taxation and Taxes in England* (first edn. 1884; third edn. 1965) vol. 2, p. 249 *et seq.* These figures

do not always agree exactly with those given in B.R. Mitchell, *British Historical Statistics* (Cambridge 1988), but the overall picture is not very different.

CHAPTER 5

1. In this chapter, as elsewhere in the book, figures are mostly taken from B.R. Mitchell, *British Historical Statistics* (Cambridge 1988), and the sources on which he draws, As the financial year ended on 5 January during the first half of the nineteenth century, figures there given of returns for a financial year mean 'year ending'. Thus, figures given under 1816 refer to what happened mainly in 1815, and so on.
2. See discussion in Lionel Munby, *How Much Is That Worth?* (Chichester 1989), and the sources to which he refers.
3. Sydney Buxton, *Finance and Politics: an Historical Study 1783–1885* (London 1888) vol. 1, p. 19.
4. Sir Stafford H. Northcote, *Twenty Years of Financial Policy* ... (London 1862).
5. *Annual Register* (1842), p. 73.
6. E. Halévy, *Victorian Years 1841–1895* (N.Y. 1961), pp. 103–21.
7. Buxton, *op. cit.*, vol. 1, p. 155.
8. Here understood to mean the total unredeemed capital.
9. Some excise receipts, e.g. licence fees, were classified by the Treasury as direct rather than indirect taxes.

CHAPTER 6

1. See discussion in Eric J. Evans, *Tithes, Maps, Apportionments and the 1836 Act* (Chichester 1993).
2. Gordon Donaldson, *Scotland, James V to James VII* (Edinburgh 1971), p. 298.
3. For discussions of tithes, see Eric J. Evans, *The Contentious Tithe* (London &c 1976); and also Evans, *op. cit.*
4. See Oliver Macdonagh article in W.E. Vaughan, ed., *A New History of Ireland: v, Ireland under the Union 1801–70* (Oxford 1989).
5. See Sidney and Beatrice Webb, *English Local Government: English Poor Law History, Part 1* (London &c., 1927), pp. 152–3.
6. Webb and Webb, *op. cit.*, part 2 (London &c., 1929), p. 2.
7. Cited in Edwin Cannan's old, but very lucid, account, *The History of Local Rates in England* (London &c., 1896).
8. Cannan, *op. cit.*, p. 94.
9. Cannan, *op. cit.*, p. 79, 81.
10. Webb and Webb, *op. cit.*, part 2, p. 3.
11. J.V. Beckett, *Local Taxation: National Legislation and the Problems of Enforcement* (London 1980).
12. Herman Finer, *English Local Government* (London 1950), p. 301.
13. See discussion in E. Halévy, *England in 1815* (London 1964), pp. 377–81.

14. For development of Scots practice, see Gordon Donaldson, *op. cit.*, and William Ferguson, *Scotland 1689 to the Present* (Edinburgh 1968). There is a useful summary of Scottish and Irish developments in Webb and Webb, *op. cit.*, part 2, pp. 1025–34.
15. S.H. Turner, The *History of Local Taxation in Scotland* (Edinburgh and London 1908) p. 41.
16. Turner, *op. cit.*, p. 27.
17. H.M. Knox, *Two Hundred and Fifty Years of Scottish Education*, 1696–1946 (Edinburgh 1953).
18. Virginia Crossman, *Local Government in 19th Century Ireland* (Belfast 1994).
19. *Annual Register* (1835).
20. George S. Pryde, *Scotland from 1603 to the Present Day* (London etc., 1962), pp. 188–95.
21. Ibid., p. 196.
22. E. Halévy, *The Triumph of Reform 1830–1841* (London 1961), pp. 214–15.

CHAPTER 7

1.   John Bright Jr and J.E. Thorold Rogers (eds), *Speeches by Richard Cobden*. (London 1870; 1908), p. 493.
2.   C.H. Feinstein, *National Income, Expenditure and Output of the U.K., 1855–1965* (Cambridge 1972).
3.   Elwood P. Lawrence, *Henry George in the British Isles* (East Lansing, Mich., 1957).
4.   R.C.K. Ensor, *England 1870–1914* (Oxford 1966), p. 334. The other references are to Laurence Gronlund, *Cooperative Commonwealth* (1884), and Edward Bellamy, *Looking Backward* (1887).
5.   See, in particular, Benjamin H. Brown, *The Tariff Reform Movement in Great Britain 1881–1895*. (N.Y. 1942).
6.   Commercial Union … 9. ii. 1890 (CAB 37/29) No. 7.
7.   A.G. Gardiner, *The Life of Sir William Harcourt* II, pp. 280–1.
8.   Bernard Mallet, *British Budgets 1887–88 to 1912–13*. (London 1913), p. 81.
9.   Ibid., pp. 74–5.
10. Bruce K. Murray, *The People's Budget 1909–10* … (Oxford 1980), p. 1.
11. Pamela Horn, *The Tithe War in Pembrokeshire* (Fishguard 1982), pp. 5–16; Roy Douglas, *Land, People and Politics* … (London 1976), pp. 99–103.
12. Étinne Martin, *Les impôts directs en Angleterre* … (Paris &c., 1905), p. 125.
13. Murray, *op. cit.*, p. 48; Douglas, *op. cit.*, pp. 118–20.
14. The history of the London coal duties was discussed in the House of Commons by Sir J. Pease. Parl. Deb. 3s. 336, (22. v. 1889).

CHAPTER 8

1.   Bernard Mallet, *British Budgets 1887–88 to 1912–13* (London 1913), provides an excellent account of public finance in the period.

2. C.T. Ritchie, *Public Finance*, 23. xii. 1902. (CAB 37/63).
3. C.T. Ritchie, *Our Financial Position*. 21. ii. 1903 (CAB 37/64).
4. See, for example, G.L.R. memorandum, 'Extension of the basis of indirect taxation' (x. 1901). (CAB 37/58), No. 93.
5. Mallet, *op. cit.*, p. 105.
6. Blain, *Direct and Indirect Taxation* [1903] (CAB 37/66) No. 61.
7. In this period, the word 'colony' was applied generally to places in the overseas British Empire, except India, but including those which were self-governing.
8. C.T. Ritchie, *Our Financial Position*, 21. ii. 1903 (CAB 37/64).
9. C.T. Ritchie memorandum, 9. ix. 1903 (CAB 37/66), No. 58.
10. A.J. Balfour, *Speeches on Fiscal Policy*, 13. x. 1903 (CAB 37/66), No. 64.
11. Many modern authorities gives the 'Labour' figures for the 1906 Election as 51 – sometimes one or two more. This number includes not only the 29 LRC members, who were committed to independent action, but also 'Liberal–Labour'– 'Labour' in the nineteenth-century sense – who took the Liberal Whip.
12. Harry Browne, in *Joseph Chamberlain, Radical and Imperialist* (London 1974) p. 72, gives the Unionist figures as: Chamberlain's supporters 109; 'Balfourites' – that is, people who were prepared to support 'retaliation' without going all the way with the 'Tariff Reformers' – 32, Unionist Free Traders 11. This leaves five Unionist MPs. unclassified; but it is important to remember that when, as here, there is a continuum of opinion, any simple classification is somewhat arbitrary.

CHAPTER 9

1. Bruce Murray, *The People's Budget 1909–10* ... (Oxford 1980) pp. 36–7.
2. *Aged Poor*. Hicks Beach, 18. xi. 1899; Balfour 12. xii. 1899 (CAB 37/51), Nos. 89, 95.
3. C.T. Ritchie, 9. ix. 1903 (CAB 37/66), No. 58.
4. See table in *Liberal Magazine* (1909), pp. 236–7.
5. For general discussions of the 'inwardness' of the budget dispute, see Murray, *op. cit.*: Geoffrey Lee, *The People's Budget: an Edwardian Tragedy* (London, 1996); Roy Jenkins: *Mr Balfour's Poodle* (London 1968).
6. Lloyd George memorandum, 29. i. 1909. (CAB 37/97), No. 16.
7. *Liberal Magazine 1909*, p. 330.
8. Murray, *op. cit.*, p. 218.
9. Kenneth Young, *Arthur James Balfour* (London 1963), pp. 289–90.
10. For analysis of the division, see *Liberal Magazine* (1909), pp. 684–5.
11. On the Second Reading division, 25. iv. 1910, 62 Irish Nationalists supported the Government, 8 voted against it and 11 were absent. *Liberal Magazine* (1910), p. 192.
12. Murray, *op. cit.*, pp. 296–7.
13. Ibid., p. 293.
14. The Report of Committee on National Debt and Taxation (Cmd. 2800 of 1927) gives some illuminating figures, pp. 94–5.

CHAPTER 10

1. McKenna memorandum, 22. vii. 1915 (CAB 37/131) No. 37; Sir John
    Bradbury memorandum 9. ix. 1915 (CAB 37/134) No. 11; J.M. Keynes, *The
    Financial Position*, 9. ix. 1915. (CAB 37/134) No. 12.
2. Balfour memorandum 17. x. 1915; Bonar Law memorandum 25. x. 1915
    (CAB 37/136), Nos. 18, 30.
3. This figure, and most other figures in this chapter, are taken from, or calcu-
    lated from, Bernard Mallet, *British Budgets 1887–88 to 1912–13* (London
    1913).
4. Chamberlain would have preferred the designation 'Unionist'; but for practi-
    cal purposes the two words meant the same thing by this date.
5. Sir Edgar Harper, *The Lloyd George Finance (1909–10) Act 1910: its errors,
    and how to correct them* (International Union for Land Value Taxation and
    Free Trade, London 1929).

CHAPTER 11

1. Keith Laybourn, *The Evolution of British Social Policy and the Welfare State*
    (Keele 1995), p. 192.
2. Sir George Mallet and C.O. George, *British Budgets, 3rd series, 1921–22 to
    1932–33* (London, 1933), Table vii.
3. Cabinet 5(32) 21. i. 1932; 6(32) 22. i. 1932 (CAB 23/70).
4. Cabinet 47(32) 28. ix. 1932 (morning), (CAB 23/72)
5. Cabinet 48(32) 28. ix. 1932 (afternoon), (CAB 23/72)

CHAPTER 12

1. The Saar is an arguable exception. The district had been placed under the
    League of Nations under the peace treaties, but provision was made for a
    plebiscite in 1935. This resulted in a large majority for return to Germany,
    which was set into effect.
2. Calculations have been made here on the basis of figures in B.R. Mitchell,
    British Historical Statistics (Cambridge 1988), many of which are based on
    C.H. Feinstein, *National Income, Expenditure and Output of the United
    Kingdom 1855–1965* (Cambridge 1972).

CHAPTER 13

1. Figures based on those given in B.R. Mitchell, *British Historical Statistics*
    (Cambridge 1988), and calculations from those figures.
2. See L.J. Tivey, *Nationalisation in British Industry* (London 1966), p. 43.
3. (CAB 129/45), fo. 20 *et seq.*
4. *IRC report for year ending 31 March 1974.* Cmd. 5804.

5. *Barclay's Bank Review May 1985*, cited in K.W. Glaister, *The Meaning, Measurement and Consequences of Inflation* (London 1987), p. 6.
6. *The Next Ten Years* ... Cmd. 9189, 1983–4.
7. Related to 1982–3 prices, central government taxes in 1963–4 had been £41.4 milliard, local government rates £6.4 milliard, NI contributions £8.3 milliard. The respective figures in 1978–9 were £69.3 milliard, £9.4 milliard and £16.8 milliard.
8. Unemployment figures based on data in *Employment Gazette*, later renamed *Labour Market Trends*. Other authorities give different figures.

CHAPTER 14

1. Margaret Thatcher, *The Downing Street Years* (London 1993), p. 7.
2. 1978–9 total tax revenue (in millions) was £40,814, the yield of Income Tax, Surtax and Corporation Tax was £22,703, and the yield of customs and excise £13,764. In 1982–3, corresponding figures were £76,295, £36,040 and £27,940. *Report of IR Commissioners July 1986*, Cmd 9831.
3. £57,136 million out of £111,704 million. *Report of IR Commissioners November 1989*. Cm. 880.
4. Nigel Lawson, *The View from No. 11: Memoirs of a Tory Radical* (London &c., 1992), p. 562.
5. Thatcher, *op. cit.*, p. 648.
6. Lawson, *op. cit.*, pp. 573–4.
7. Thatcher, *op. cit.*, p. 652.
8. *Annual Register* 1990, p. 17.
9. Lawson, *op. cit.*, p. 583.
10. Figures based on those given in *Annual Register*, and calculations therefrom.
11. *Annual Register* figures are: 1978–9: taxes on income £25,075; VAT £4,832; 1995–6: taxes on income £92,956; VAT £43,073.

CHAPTER 15

1. *Accounts & Papers* 19, 1874 (liii).

Bibliography

Annual Register

Ashley, Maurice, *England in the 17th Century (1603–1714)*. Pelican, Harmondsworth, 1952.

Baxter, Stephen B., *The Development of the Treasury 1660–1702*. Longman Green & Co., London etc., 1957.

Becker, Robert A., *Revolution, Reform and the Politics of American Taxation 1763–1783*. Louisiana State University Press, 1980.

Beckett, J.V., 'Land Tax or Excise: the levying of taxation in seventeenth- and eighteenth-century England, *Eng. Hist. Review* c (1985) pp. 284–308.

Beckett, J.V., *Local Taxation*. Published for Standing Conference for Local History by Bedford Square Press, 1980.

Bellamy, Edward, *Looking Backward 2000–1887*. Tickner & Co., Boston, 1888.

Binney, J.E.D., *British Public Finance and Administration 1774–92*. Oxford University Press, 1958.

Bowley, Arthur L., *The Change in the Distribution of the National Income 1880–1913*. Clarendon Press, Oxford, 1920.

Braddick, M.J., *Parliamentary Taxation in Seventeenth-Century England*. Royal Historical Society/Boydell Press, 1994.

Braddick, J.J., *The Nerves of State: Taxation and the Financing of the English State, 1558–1714*. Manchester University Press, 1996.

Brewer, John, *The Sinews of Power: War, Money and the English State 1688–1783*. Unwin Hyman, 1989.

Brisco, Norris A., *The Economic Policy of Robert Walpole*. Columbia University Press, New York, 1907.

Brodrick, G.C. and Fotheringham, J.K., *History of England... 1801–1837*. AMS Press Kraus Reprint Co., New York, 1969.

Brown, Benjamin H., *The Tariff Reform Movement in Great Britain 1881–1895*. Columbia University Press, New York, 1943.

Browne, Harry, *Joseph Chamberlain, Radical and Imperialist*. Longman, London, 1974.

Bullion, John L., *A Great and Necessary Measure: George Grenville and the Genesis of the Stamp Act 1763–1765*. University of Missouri Press, 1982.

Buxton, Sydney, *Finance and Politics: An Historical Study 1783–1885*. 2 vols. John Murray, London, 1888.

Cabinet Memoranda. CAB 37. Public Record Office, Kew, Surrey.

Cannan, Edwin, *The History of Local Rates in England*. Longman Green & Co., London & c. 1896.

Chandaman, C.D., *The English Public Revenue 1660–1688*. Oxford University Press, 1975.

Clark, Sir George, *The Later Stuarts 1660–1714*. Oxford University Press, 1985 edn.

Coffield, James, *A Popular History of Taxation*. Longman, London, 1970.

Comerford, R.V. 'Churchmen, Tenants and Independent Opposition 1850–56'. In Vaughan, W.E., ed., *A New History of Ireland*. Vol. 5: *Ireland Under The Union I. 1801–70*. Clarendon Press, Oxford.

Cook, Chris, and Brendon, Keith, *British Historical Facts 1830–1900*. Macmillan, London, 1975.

Crossman, Virginia, *Local Government in 19th Century Ireland*. Institute of Irish Studies (QUB) for the Ulster Society of Irish Historical Studies 1994.

Davies, Godfrey, *The Early Stuarts 1603–1660*. Oxford University Press, 1959 edn.

Dickson, P.G.M., *The Financial Revolution in England 1688–1756*. Macmillan, London, 1967.

Dictionary of National Biography.

Donaldson, Gordon, *Scotland, James V James VII*. Oliver & Boyd, Edinburgh, 1971.

Douglas, Roy, *Land, People and Politics: A History of the Land Question in the United Kingdom, 1878–1952*. Allison & Busby, London, 1976.

Dowell, Stephen, *A History of Taxation and Taxes in England*. 4 vols. Frank Cass & Co., London. First edn. 1884; third edn. 1965.

Dutton, David, *Austen Chamberlain: Gentleman in Politics*. Ross Anderson Publications, 1985.

Employment Gazette, later *Labour Market Trends*.

Encyclopaedia Britannica.

Evans, Eric J., *The Contentious Tithe: The Tithe Problem and English Agriculture 1750–1850*. Routledge & Kegan Paul, London & c., 1976.

Evans, Eric J., *Tithes, Maps, Apportionments and the 1836 Act*. Phillimore, for British Association for Local History. Chichester, 1993.

Everyman's Encyclopaedia.

Feinstein, C.H., *National Income, Expenditure and Output of the United Kingdom 1855–1965*, Cambridge University Press, 1972.

Ferguson, William, *Scotland 1689 to the Present*. Oliver & Boyd, Edinburgh, 1968.

Finlayson, Geoffrey, *Citizen, State and Social Welfare in Britain 1830–1990*. Clarendon Press, Oxford, 1994.

Gardiner, A.G., *The Life of Sir William Harcourt*. Constable & Co. Ltd., London, 1923.

Gilbert, Bentley B., *The Evolution of National Insurance in Great Britain: The Origins of the Welfare State*. Gregg Revivals, 1993 reprint.

Glaister, K.W., *The Meaning, Measurement and Consequences of Inflation*. Longman Economic Series, 1987.

Gribbon, H.D., 'Economic and Social History 1850–1921: In Vaughan, W.E., ed., *A New History of Ireland*, VI, ii. 1870–1921. Clarendon Press, Oxford, 1996.

Gronlund, Lawrence, *The Cooperative Commonwealth*. Swan, Sonnenschein, Le Bas & Lawrey, London, 1884.

Groves, Harold M., *Tax Philosophers*. University of Wisconsin Press, 1974.

Halévy, E., *History of the English People in the 19th Century*. Vols 1 to 6. Ernest Benn Ltd., London, 1961.

Harper, Sir Edgar, *The Lloyd George Finance (1909–10) Act, 1910: Its Errors and How to Correct Them*. International Union for Land Value Taxation and Free Trade, 1929.

Hill, Brian W., *Sir Robert Walpole*. Hamish Hamilton, London, 1989.

Hill, Christopher, *The Century of Revolution 1603–1714*. Thomas Nelson & Sons Ltd, Walton-on-Thames, 1980 edn.

Horn, Pamela, *The Tithe War in Pembrokeshire*. Preseli Printers, Fishguard, 1982.

Horowitz, *Henry, Parliament, Policy and Politics in the Reign of William III.* Manchester University Press, 1977.

Hughes, Edward, *Studies in Administration and Finance 1558–1825.* Manchester University Press, 1934.

Hunt, William, *History of England ... 1760–1801.* Longman Green, 1905. Reprint 1969.

Hyde, H. Montgomery, *Neville Chamberlain.* Weidenfeld & Nicolson, London, 1976.

Jenkins, Roy (Lord Jenkins of Hillhead), *Mr. Balfour's Poodle.* Collins, London, 1968.

Jones, D.W., *War and Economy in the Age of William III and Marlborough.* Basil Blackwell, Oxford, 1988.

Keesing's Contemporary Archives.

Kemp, Betty, *Sir Robert Walpole.* Weidenfeld & Nicolson, London, 1976.

Kennedy, William, *English Taxation 1640–1799.* G. Bell & Sons Ltd, London, 1913.

Kenyon, J.P., *Stuart England.* Pelican, Harmondsworth, 1978.

Knox, H.M., *Two Hundred and Fifty Years of Scottish Education 1696–1946.* Oliver & Boyd, Edinburgh, 1953.

Lawson, Nigel, *The View From No. 11: Memoirs of a Tory Radical.* Bantam Press, London etc., 1992.

Laybourn, Keith, *The Evolution of British Social Policy and the Welfare State.* Ryburn Publishing, Keele University Press, 1995.

Liberal Magazine. Liberal Publication Department, London.

Liberal Pamphlets and Leaflets. Liberal Publication Department, London.

Lodge, Richard, *The History of England from the Restoration to the Death of William III.* Longmans Green & Co, London, etc., 1910; AMS Press Kraus Reprint Co., New York, 1969.

Low, Sidney and Sanders, Lloyd C., *Political History of England 1837–1901.* AMS Press. Kraus Reprint Co., New York, 1969.

Macdonagh, Oliver, 'The Economy and Society 1830–45'. In Vaughan, W.E., ed., *A New History of Ireland,* vol. V. Clarendon Press, Oxford, 1989.

McDowell, R.B., 'Revolution and the Union 1794–1800'. In Moody, T.W. and Vaughan, W.E., eds., *A New History of Ireland,* vol. IV. Clarendon Press, Oxford, 1986.

McDowell, R.B., 'Administration and the Public Services 1870–1921'. In Vaughan, W.E., ed., *A New History of Ireland,* vol. VI. Clarendon Press, Oxford, 1996.

McKenna, Stephen, *Reginald McKenna 1863–1943.* Eyre & Spottiswoode, London, 1948.

Mallet, (Sir) Bernard, *British Budgets 1887–88 to 1912–13.* Macmillan, London, 1913.

Mallet, (Sir) Bernard and George, C. Oswald, *British Budgets* 2nd Series: *1913–14 to 1920–21.* Macmillan, London, 1929.

Mallet, Sir Bernard and George, C. Oswald, *British Budgets* 3rd Series: *1921–22 to 1932–33.* Macmillan, London, 1933.

Martin, Étienne, *Les Impôts Directs en Angleterre: Taxes Locales et Impériales.* Berger-Levrault et Cie, Paris et Nancy, 1905.

Millard, P.W., *Tithes and Variable Rent Charges: Some Aspects of Their History and Development.* Butterworth, London, 1933.

Mitchell, B.R, *British Historical Statistics.* Cambridge University Press, 1988.

Montague, F.C., *The History of England from the Accession of James I to the Restoration*. Longmans Green & Co, London, etc., 1907; AMS Press Kraus Reprint Co., New York, 1969.

Murray, Bruce K., *The People's Budget 1909/10: Lloyd George and Liberal Politics*. Clarendon Press, Oxford, 1980.

Northcote, Sir Stafford H., *Twenty Years of Fiscal Policy ... 1842–1861*. Saunders, Otley & Co., London, 1862.

O'Brien, Patrick, 'The Political Economy of British Taxation 1660–1815'. *Econ. Hist. Rev.* 2nd ser. xli, 1988.

Ogg, David, *England in the Reign of Charles II*. 2nd edn. Oxford University Press, 1956.

Ogg, David, *England in the Reigns of James II and William III*. Oxford University Press, 1984.

Peters, B. Guy, *The Development of the Tax State*. Centre for the Study of Public Policy, Glasgow, 1985.

Pryde, George S., *Scotland from 1603 to the Present Day*. Thomas Nelson & Sons Ltd., London & c., 1962.

The Radical Programme. With a preface by J. Chamberlain. Chapman & Hall, London, 1885.

Rawcliffe, Michael, *The Welfare State*. Dryad Press, London, 1990.

Redlich, Josef and Hirst, Francis W., *The History of Local Government in England*. Macmillan, London, 1958.

Report of Committee on National Debt and Taxation. Cmd. 2800 of 1927.

Riddell, George H. (Lord Riddell), *More pages from My Diary 1908–1914*. Country Life Ltd., London, 1934.

Roseveare, Henry, *The Financial Revolution 1660–1760*. Longmans, London, etc., 1991.

Roseveare, Henry, *The Treasury 1660–1870*. George Allen & Unwin, London, 1973.

Sabine, B.E.V., *A Short History of Taxation*. Butterworths, London, 1980.

Self, Robert C., *Tories and Tariffs: the Conservative Party and the Policies of Tariff Reform 1922–1932*. Garland Publishing Inc., N.Y. and London, 1986.

Seligman, Edwin R., *The Income Tax*. Macmillan, N.Y., 1911.

Sinclair, Cecil, *Tracing Scottish Local History*. Scottish Record Office, Edinburgh, 1994.

Socialism Made Plain: Being the Social and Political Manifesto of the Democratic Federation. June 1883.

Thatcher, Margaret, *The Downing Street Years*. Harper Collins, London, 1993.

Timmins, Nicholas, *The Five Giants: a Biography of the Welfare State*. HarperCollins, London, 1995.

Tivey, L.J., *Nationalisation in British Industry*. Jonathan Cape, London, 1966.

Turner, S.H., *The History of Local Taxation in Scotland*. William Blackwood & Sons, Edinburgh and London, 1908.

Wallace, Alfred Russel, *Land Nationalisation, its Necessity and its Aims*. Trübner & Co., London, 1882.

Ward, W.R., 'The Administration of the Window and Assessed Taxes 1696–1798. *Eng. Hist. Review* lxii (1952) pp. 522–42.

Ward, W.R., *The English Land Tax in the Eighteenth Century*. Oxford University Press, 1953.

Webb, Sidney and Beatrice, *English Local Government: English Poor Law History*. Part 1: *The Old Poor Law*. Longman Green, London & c., 1927.

Webb, Sidney and Beatrice, *English Local Government: English Poor Law History*. Part 2: *The Last Hundred Years*. Longman Green. London & c., 1929.

Western, J.R., *Monarchy and Revolution: The English State in the 1680s*. Blandford Press, London, 1971.

Woodward, Sir Llewellyn, *The Age of Reform*. Oxford University Press, 1962.

Young, Kenneth, *Arthur James Balfour... 1848–1930*. G. Bell & Sons, Ltd, London, 1963.

Index

.

DATE DUE